M000007672

The Ponemah Years

WALKING IN THE FOOTSTEPS OF MY MOTHER

Bernice L. Rocque

3HOUSES

Trumbull, Connecticut
www.3Houses.com

The Ponemah Years: Walking in the Footsteps of My Mother

Copyright © 2017 by Bernice L. Rocque. All rights reserved.

Published by 3Houses

Except for brief quotations in articles or reviews, no part of this book may be reproduced or transmitted in any form or by any means, electronic or mechanical, or by any information and retrieval system, without prior written permission from the publisher. The contact information is:

3Houses, P.O. Box 604, Trumbull, CT

Email: BLR@3Houses.com

Cover and interior design: Diane King, dkingdesigner.com

ISBN 978-0-9856822-5-5 (Paperback)

First Edition: November 2017

This is dedicated to
my mother Gabrielle and
to my grandmother Eugenie.
In seeing the essence of our mothers –
we see ourselves.

Preface

I have been hooked on genealogy since my 5th grade teacher Mrs. Parkhurst gave an assignment to talk to our parents and grandparents, and fill out a family tree chart. When that door opened for me around 1960 at Samuel Huntington School in Norwichtown, Connecticut, my mission became to find the connections between my family's past and present people. This beautiful odyssey has no end, just infinite discovery.

This book evolved from a walk with my mother, Gabrielle Picard Janovicz. She and I attended a WALK-TOBER tour in Fall 2004, led by Mr. Rene Dugas, Sr. In 2005, I prepared an article for the *Norwich Bulletin* about what we took away from that walk through Taftville, Connecticut—and her return after more than 50 years to the grounds of the Ponemah Mill.

In 2014, I became aware that Taftville Fire Chief Tim Jencks was scheduled to lead an encore WALK-TOBER tour of the Mill. I decided to drive to Taftville because that tour would include the *inside* of Ponemah's Main Building and a few other structures in the rear courtyard.

Following the WALKTOBER tours, I conversed with my mother and other relatives about the time when they or members of their family worked in this giant fabric mill. The 2014 blog piece on my author site reflects how my knowledge deepened beyond family tree research. That article became the start point for this book.

In the past decade or so, I have veered away from extending my tree and concentrated, instead, on sitting in the light of a particular time period. What was life like for my family's cast of characters? *Until the Robin Walks on Snow*, my first book, reflects this switch to traveling deep instead of broad in my family history research pattern.

This volume is part biography, part history, part memoir, and part family portrait. In telling my mother's story, the narrative weaves between periods in the past and present, traversing back and forth, over and over—moving much like the shuttle in the looms my mother operated at the Ponemah Mill.

Fundamentally, my mother's story is about rising above extreme loss and navigating towards a better life. I hope her story opens a window in your own world, while you learn about periods of time during the Mill's first one hundred years. For anyone with heritage roots here, we feel the hope, don't we? The majestic Ponemah Mill sits on the threshold of its next life.

The Ponemah Mill and its village. Taftville, Connecticut.

Table of Contents

Introduction

Ponemah Mill
Building No. 1.

My mother loved her weaving job at the Ponemah Mill.

I didn't learn this until late in my mother's life. There were little clues now and then, but I didn't see or hear them, even as a budding genealogist. When I was growing up, we drove past the giant building frequently, yet Mom rarely mentioned the Mill, and I didn't ask her about the time when she worked. My mother and I lost precious conversations we could have had, when her reservoir of memories was fuller.

This early 1940s photo of my mother Gabrielle Picard was taken in the backyard of her family's home during the years she worked at the Ponemah

Gabrielle Picard, early 1940s.

Mill in Taftville, a section of Norwich, Connecticut. The building rising in the photo's background was part of the mill complex.

After my dad died in 2001, Mom wanted to talk more about her childhood and her life before they married. Unlike many women coming of age during WWII, she did not leave her job once she married, or even a year later in June 1946, when Dad returned from wartime service in the Marines.

Dad was a practical man. Why should she leave her job if she wanted to work? To them, it didn't matter what other people were doing. It was a philosophy drilled into my sisters and me when we were growing up.

Michael Janovicz, circa 1943.

Like many Post-War couples, they lived for a while with each of their families, but they wanted a place of their own. My parents' goal was to build a house that was mortgage free, not a common status at the time.

Mom's job at the Mill had begun purely as a monetary decision by her father, much like the decision her parents made to leave their dairy farm in Canada. The farm's income was not enough to support them, so my mother's parents emigrated to the U.S. for the fair wages and steady work offered by the famous Ponemah Mill. Like many families of the time, my mother and her siblings would go to work early in their lives.

Part One

The Picard Family Arrives in Taftville

My mother was four years old when her family took "the long train ride" from Montreal to Connecticut. They traveled with a friend, Esdras Daignault, and entered the U.S. in Vermont in May 1924. The family stayed for a week with a distant relative of Eugenie's before renting a four-bedroom duplex on South A Street.

My grandmother, Eugenie, had convinced her husband Alphonse Picard to come to the United States, and specifically to Taftville, the location of the Ponemah Mill, then in its operational heyday. My

grandparents made the move when they were in their early 40s, with 12 children. The 1920s were a time of prosperity in the U.S., but despite having owned a farm in Canada, Alphonse had to borrow money from Eugenie's mother to finance the trip.

Actually, my grandmother Eugenie Duhamel was born in the United States in Slatersville, Rhode Island, to French-Canadian parents. Samuel Slater had revolutionized the production of cotton textiles in the U.S. by applying new technology and management techniques in New England's earliest fabric mills in the Blackstone River Valley in Massachusetts and in Rhode Island, where Eugenie's father Louis Duhamel worked.

My great-grandparents would return to Canada when my grandmother Eugenie was thirteen. In 1894, they combined a retirement decision with a move intended to control their youngest daughter. To Eugenie's surprise—her parents carried out their threat

◀ *Eugenie, Alphonse, and her mother Louise at the Duhamel home in St. Theodore, Quebec, circa 1920.*

Eugenie Duhamel, circa 1890.

Louise Beaudoin and her daughters. ▶

to send her to a con-vent school in Canada in order to separate her and a young man with whom she was smitten!

Sadly, Louis Duhamel died in 1895, about a year after he and his wife Louise returned to Canada. This photo (above right) shows Louise in what appears to be mourning attire, with her daughters. His death may have profoundly affected his youngest daughter, Eugenie, because after her schooling….at the Acton Vale Convent was completed, she decided to remain, and enter the Convent to become a nun.

The Picard and Duhamel families lived within a half-mile of each other, along the same road in St. Theodore d'Acton, a small town out-side Montreal. (See the diagram.) It seems likely that, as neighbors, Alphonse and Eugenie knew each other as they were coming of age. He was six years older than Eugenie. Perhaps he noticed that she was blossoming into an attractive young woman.

Somehow, Eugenie and Alphonse became better acquainted while she was a novitiate at the Acton Vale Convent, located about five miles from St. Theodore. How their paths crossed on a regular basis is unclear, but my working theory is that his family's farm delivered dairy products to the Convent.

When I interviewed my relatives in the 1970s, they described Eugenie as a gentle, soft-spoken, and cheerful person. According to Aunt Flor-ence, Alphonse begged Eugenie, again and again, to marry him instead of becoming a nun. She finally accepted his proposal, despite objec-tions from her upper middle-class family. They found Alphonse unsuitable, possi-bly because as one of the youngest, he would not inherit his family's farm.

Eugenie's family could have objected to the marriage for a second reason. My mother told me the Roman Catholic Church, at this time, expected

Alphonse Picard, circa 1888.

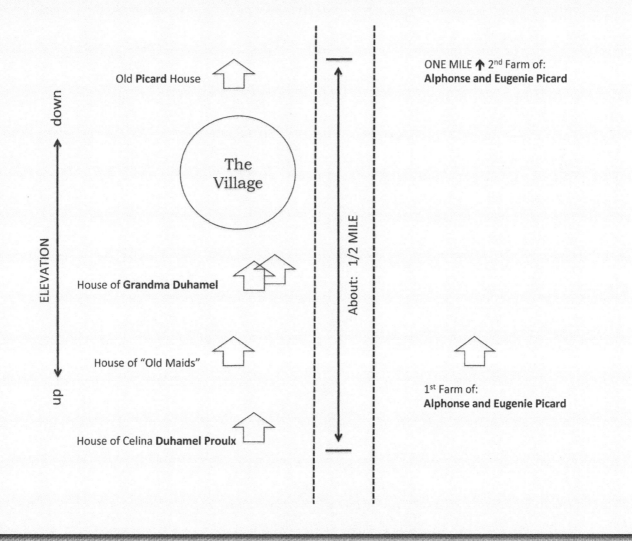

Proximity of Picard and Duhamel families in St. Theodore d'Acton, Quebec, Canada – Map circa 1924.

large French-Canadian families to offer up one child, upon reaching adulthood, for the priesthood or convent. Eugenie's decision to leave the convent likely caused embarrassment for her family.

A generation later, one of Eugenie's children would respond to the calling, entering the convent in September 1932. My mother's sister, Rita, took her vows in May 1937, becoming Sister Marie Alphonsia.

All the nuns shared in the work of the convent and soon they were utilizing the sewing talent of my aunt, possibly cultivated by her father Alphonse. He worked as a farmhand at the Ponemah Farm during the 1920s and 1930s and in his elder years had worked as a night watchman for the Mill. My mother told me her father had worked as a tailor, too, perhaps while living in Canada.

When my sisters and I were growing up, our family visited Sr. Alphonsia now and then on Sunday afternoons at the Academy of the Holy Family in Baltic, sometimes in tandem with my Picard cousins from Taftville. I think the nuns thought of us as a rambunctious whirlwind of joyful noise and activity! It was a tight squeeze of bodies in that small parlor, so sometimes, while the adults talked, my cousin Susie and I would slip away through the glass doors and explore the convent.

Sr. Alphonsia lived to be 97-years-old—so far the longest life among Mom's siblings. At her funeral service, a representative

▲ *Sunday Visits to the Convent .*

from the Norwich Diocese shared memories about my aunt and her contributions as a seamstress. She had sewn many a Mass vestment during her assignment at the Bishop's House. We learned that as far as my aunt was concerned, if there was a ripple where there shouldn't be one, the item needed to be fixed.

An easy-going extravert most of the time, my aunt could reveal a hidden assertiveness—when she needed it! Humorous anecdotes about Sister Alphonsia, holding her ground against the ecclesiastical establishment, brought smiles from me and from the others attending her memorial service. I found myself nodding. Both my mother's similar perfectionist nature and underlying

◀ *Sister Marie Alphonsia (Aunt Rita).*

will had accompanied me throughout my childhood, and into my own work life.

I recall my mother guiding me as I sewed my very first garment, a corduroy jumper. I was twelve and a member of the first class to attend two full years at the new Kelly Junior High in Norwich. The zipper was off about 3/8 inch, meaning the two sides did not align at the neckline. The memory is so clear still: me protesting about ripping out the stitching and trying to convince my mother that no one would notice the alignment issue amidst this busy hound's-tooth print.

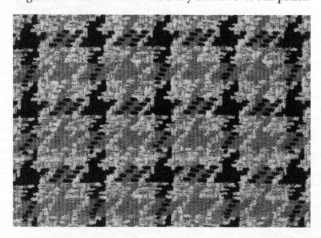

My mother's response: "Whether they see it or not, YOU will know." She told me it was my decision. I resisted for a while...and then redid it.

My two sisters and I would acknowledge that my mother's coaching about how to do things, reinforced by my dad's precision in both carpentry and his creative pursuits, shaped three organized perfectionists. Additionally, our two parents were ace project managers. Voila...three daughters with project skills at a young age!

In my experience, the processes of researching, remembering, and conversing about family history magnify what we notice accidentally about the essence of the people in our family circles—and ultimately about ourselves.

My maternal French Canadian and my paternal Eastern European ancestors left their homelands about a hundred years ago and became immigrants, starting a new life in the United States. I have tried to appreciate what that meant emotionally to them and their children. Both my mother and father learned English as a second language when they started school. Imagine the experience of being a small child sitting in a classroom, and not understanding most English words for weeks or months!

My mother's family has a long history of new starts. During a genealogy-focused vacation in the 1980s, I read the names of the founders of Quebec City on the Louis Hebert monument in the small park above the Old Town, across from the Chateau Frontenac hotel and in view of the St. Lawrence River. I was delighted to see some of my mother's ancestors listed, such as Noel Langlois, Mathurine Robin, and Jean Nicolet.

Philip Destroismaisons dit Picard, the direct paternal line French ancestor, arrived in Canada in the early 1600s. My grandmother Eugenie Duhamel descends from Thomas Duhamel dit Sanfacon, another early French settler in Canada.

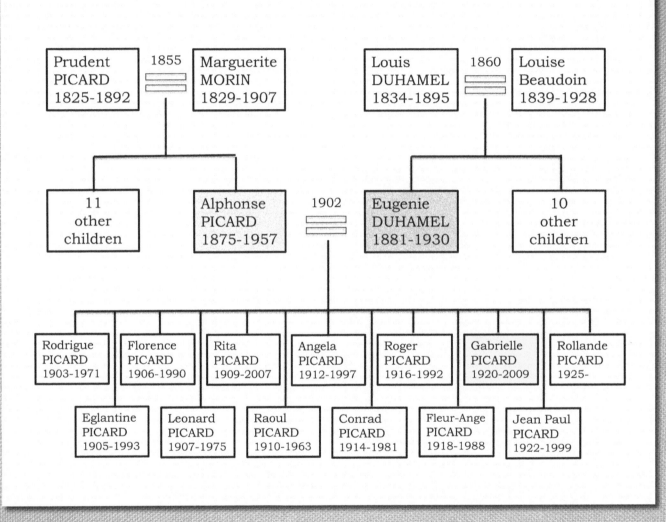

Simplified Picard/Duhamel Family Tree – 3 Generations.

◄ *Earliest Settlers of Quebec City.*

Alphonse and Eugenie Duhamel Picard, circa 1902. ►

Alphonse's father Prudent Picard, considered a "pioneer" in this Canadian local history text, left the Quebec City area in the 1850s and became one of the founding fathers of St. Theodore d'Acton, a small town outside Montreal.

Married in 1902, my grandparents Alphonse and Eugenie lived the dairy farming life of his family while welcoming a new child every year or two. This photo was likely taken early in their marriage.

The family portrait (next page) of Alphonse, Eugenie, and their thirteen surviving children was taken around 1926. My mother Gabrielle is sitting in the front row, second from the left.

My grandmother Eugenie bore seventeen children between 1902 and 1930. French-Canadian families of this time were, indeed, large. Both Alphonse and Eugenie grew up in families of greater than ten children.

Only the youngest child, Rollande, in my grandmother's arms, was born in the U.S. At this writing, Aunt Rollie, born in 1925, is the only family member in this photo still living.

My grandmother Eugenie died in 1930 when my mother was ten. Mom remembered her as a gentle and soft-spoken woman. My mother's most enduring memory was sitting on her mother's lap and being held close to her.

▲ *The Picard Family, circa 1926.*
Top Row L-R: Florence, Rita, Leonard, Rodrigue, Ida, Ralph.
Bottom Row L-R: Roger, Gabrielle, Eugenie holding Rollie, Jean Paul, Alphonse, Floy, Conrad, Angela.

When I translated a letter my grandmother had written home during her visit to Canada in July 1928, I discovered Eugenie could be quite funny.

In a light-hearted narrative, my grandmother replied with humor to Florence's news that young Jean Paul, six years old, was throwing daily tantrums in Taftville because he wanted his mother, and she was not there.

Eugenie also relayed back to Aunt Florence a recent story of how little Rollie, nearly 3 years old, had wandered into another

room, found a pair of scissors, and cut off much of her own hair! The Canadian relatives were not amused, unlike my grandmother.

I find her mood in this letter amazing, considering Aunt Florence told me my grandmother traveled home to Canada in 1928 with somewhat a heavy heart. Eugenie was ill. She wanted her family to meet her youngest child, Rollande, born since the family had left Canada. My great grandmother Marie Louise Beaudoin Duhamel

◀ *Eugenie and Rollie in Canada, July 1928.*

◀ Rollie and doll in Canada, July 1928.

Aunt Ida and first husband Paul Miclette, circa 1926. ▶

may have been in poor health that summer, too, as she died in December, six months after her daughter Eugenie's visit.

When my mother's eldest sister Ida reflected about the years she was growing up in Canada, she felt her widowed, but financially comfortable Duhamel grandmother was somewhat "stingy." When she sent her grandchildren to the store to buy penny candy, she would give them the exact number of pennies, and once they returned, she did not share the candy with them. This did not endear her to her grandchildren. With the mischief renewed in Aunt Ida's eyes, she added that they used to play tricks on "the old girl."

Grandmother Louise would spend December to March with her daughter, Eugenie, son-in-law Alphonse and the family. In the good weather, she expected the older Picard girls

to stay with her overnight, because she didn't like being alone.

People do tend to be consistent in their behaviors over their lifetime, don't they? My great-grandmother Louise must have told her other children prior to her death that Alphonse and Eugenie still owed her money for the family's trip to the U.S. four years earlier. So, within months of my grandmother's return home to Taftville, in what turned out to be the final year of her life, Eugenie received a package from Canada after her mother died. Aunt Florence said the note indicated this was Eugenie's share of the inheritance. Inside were what Aunt Florence called "rags"—they had mailed Eugenie worn blankets and faded sheets.

While in Canada, Eugenie had consulted with her sister Celina's husband, a medical doctor named Esdras Proulx. In the years I was growing up, my mother and her family said that Eugenie died from tuberculosis. However, when I conducted my initial genealogy interviews in the 1970s, Aunt

Some of the Picard children in Canada, circa 1920. Photo likely taken a few months after my mother's birth. Back row L-R: Florence, Rita, Ida, Floy. Front row L-R: Roger, Conrad, Angela. ▶

A LA DOUCE MEMOIRE DE

Mde Eugenie Duhamel

Epouse de Alphonse Picard
décédé à Taftville. Conn. le 7 Mai 1930
à l'âge de 48 ans et 11 mois.

Je meurs, cher époux et chers enfants,
pensez à moi dans mon tombeau comme vous pen-
siez à moi sur la terre.

Je vous en supplie, ne m'oubliez jamais, restez
unis entre vous, demeurez inébranlables dans la foi.

Mes enfants soyez la consolation de votre père et
marchez toujours dans le chemin de la vertu et de
l'honnêteté.

O mon Dieu bénissez ma famille et soyez le pro-
tecteur de mes enfants.

J'implore les prières et les bonnes oeuvres de
ceux qui m'ont connue et de tous ceux que j'ai
aimés.

O bon Jésus, donnez-lui le repos
éternel.   (7 ans, 7 quar.)
Une communion, une prière, s. v. p

MADE IN FRANCE

◀ Eugenie Duhamel Picard's Death Card.

Picard family in Taftville, Connecticut at the 1938 wedding of Florence to Maurice Provencher. From left: Jean Paul, Conrad, Ralph, Gabrielle (my mother), Rollie, Ida, Florence (the bride, with hat), Leonard, Roger. ▶

Florence told me she was by the bedside of my grandmother Eugenie when she died, and shared with me that my grandmother was hemorrhaging at the end.

Only a few years ago did I check her death certificate on record in the Norwich City Clerk's office. TB was actually a secondary cause of her death. The primary cause of death was a tumor in her "stomach."

Eugenie wanted her children to complete high school. At one point, she also expressed to her husband her desire to work at the Mill. Alphonse didn't support her in either of her wishes. When she passed away just before her 49th birthday, and just after the financial crash leading to the Great Depression, those dreams for her children and for herself died with her.

After their mother died, Mom's second eldest sister Florence, then age 24, took care of the entire family and managed the large household until she married in 1938. The city directories for Norwich indicate Aunt Florence also held a job as a weaver at Ponemah during much of this 1930-38 period.

Someone needed to assume the management of the household. At least eight family members still lived at home. Her father Alphonse asked my mother Gabrielle, age 18, to accept this responsibility. ■

The Ponemah Years 1935-1950

Ponemah Mill Building No. 1
Shift Change, 1940.

Graduation

My mother's view of herself would be forever shaped by both her gratitude at attaining graduation from the 8th grade, and her discomfort at only graduating from the 8th grade.

In this picture from 1935, I see a young woman who wanted to look her best on this special day, and who held her diploma with pride. She often stated with regret that she was one of only three of their family's thirteen children to graduate from grammar school.

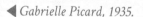
Gabrielle Picard, 1935.

L-R: Joe and Bea Jackson, Lorene and Joe Woyasz, 1985. Mom met the two sisters at the Ponemah Mill and stayed in touch with them until the end of their lives. ▶

My mother helped out at home following graduation. Her Social Security card, issued 12-29-36 indicates that her employer's name was Ponemah Mills. This document and the mention by close friends, Bea and Joe Jackson, that they met my mother at the Mill in 1937 led me to think she began to work at Ponemah that year.

Mom would work at the Mill from 1937-1950, except for a 2-year break in the mid-1940s.

After the 1938 Hurricane

The Hurricane of 1938 toppled just about every large tree in Taftville, tearing out an important physical attribute of the village in a matter of hours. In the years that followed, people who experienced the weather on September 21, 1938 could tell you exactly where they were when they realized the day had mutated into a dangerous storm, and how they navigated around debris and sometimes flooding to get back to their respective homes.

In my mother's case, she worked her shift and was at home on South A Street by mid-afternoon, as the storm's intensity increased. Knowing my mother, I expect she was relieved that she wasn't out in the worst of it, but she was worrying about those who were. The prior spring, when her older sister Florence married, her father had asked Mom, then 18, to take on the management of the household.

My mother recalled her father asking why she wasn't starting dinner. Mom said she paused in amazement before replying, "Pa, I'm not lighting the stove tonight. We're having a hurricane!"

Taftville residents, my mother told me, experienced a sickening sort of sadness when they ventured outside after the storm passed. Fallen trees, sprawled and broken, with their gnarled "feet" up, lay like bodies across every Taftville Street.

Days of steady rain ahead of the hurricane had soaked the root systems of trees across the region and filled Norwich's three rivers (the Yantic, Shetucket, and Quinebaug) to flood stage. My uncle Tony, working that day at the Norwich Free Academy print shop told

me they watched the trees at the edge of the campus plunge to the ground, one after another. The hurricane winds did howl that day—but in this particular storm the winds were not the primary reason so many trees fell across southern New England.

Some trees fell onto houses in the village. This was the scene at the South A Street duplex house where the Picard family lived. I think this photo below, shot a few days later is a testament to how well the village houses were constructed.

The destruction was overwhelming to my mother. A neighbor attempted to cheer her up and did get my mother to laugh for the first picture. The older woman who took these two photos wrote on the second photo, "You know, Gabrielle, you should face the camera and smile!! Because your smile is so nice."

It was in the month or so following the 1938 Hurricane that my parents' lives would intersect. One day, my father Michael Janovicz and a friend drove to Taftville to visit my mother's sister, Fleur-Ange, or Floy, as she was known. Mike's buddy had met Floy and was dropping by to say hello.

Floy's slightly younger sister just happened to be sitting on the front step when the two young men arrived. The strong resemblance between the sisters may have confused Mike's buddy for a moment, but my father's attention was fixed, anyway, on the shy sister named Gabrielle.

My mother's sister, Floy, seems an enigma in our Picard family's cast of characters. According to some family members, she was charming and capable; others witnessed violent reactive behavior from her at times. It is one of the greatest ironies in my mother's young life that the sister she tangled with for years would unintentionally connect Mom with the love of her life—and then, in a display of extreme behavior several years later, again advance my mother's life in a positive direction.

◀ *Fleur-Ange (Floy) Picard, circa 1940.*

Both eighteen when they met, Mike and Gay (his favored nickname for Gabrielle) dated until October 1940, when he enlisted in the Marines. At that time, Americans generally felt our entry into WWII was inevitable. I once asked Dad why he enlisted before war was declared, since all evidence suggests he was crazy about my mother. So, why leave? He told me he hated his job at United Metal Manufacturing Co., where he repaired and maintained lathes, drill presses, planers, etc. He also wasn't hopeful of getting a more challenging job. He envisioned a different future that offered more. Dad and Herb Bushnell, a boyhood friend, would talk often about the houses they would design and build.

I think there were additional reasons he enlisted. In his high school yearbook, the caption said Michael Janovicz wanted to see the world. On his enlistment papers he indicated he could speak, read, and write Polish. In 1939, Germany had invaded Poland, the homeland of his father, and I would hazard a guess that he and his family were worried. Would Germany also invade Lithuania, where his mother's family lived? His grandfather, Nikodimas, a beloved person in his childhood, had returned to Lithuania in the late 1920s. My father may have hoped for an assignment in Eastern Europe, if war was declared. Ultimately, the Marines did assign him to the European Theatre.

◀ *Michael Janovicz (far right) enlists in the Marines Corp. October 1940.*

World War II

From what they both shared about these years, it seems that Mike and Gay had agreed to date others while he was away in the service. After Marine Corp. basic training in late 1940, Dad was assigned to the Brooklyn Navy Yard for eighteen months, so he saw Gay periodically.

Meanwhile, my mother advanced in her work at the Ponemah Mill from a battery hand to a weaver, while continuing to manage her family's household. Mom dated, but told me these men paled in comparison to Mike. In February 1941, my mother and her brother Roger filed their declarations to become citizens.

Mike and Gay remained on each other's minds. In August 1941, she accompanied his family when they visited him in New York. Apparently, the visit to Bronx Park imprinted lots of

◀ *Mary, Vee, Gay, and Tony visit Mike, August 1941.*

good memories. Dad's mother brought a basket of fried chicken and other favorite foods of her son for everyone to enjoy. Dad's brother Tony and sister Vee, both in their 90s now, still remember the day.

The reunions became less frequent after the bombing of Pearl Harbor in December 1941. Beginning in July 1942, my father spent eighteen months in Iceland as the Gun Captain, during which he and a small group of Marines spotted and shot down a German Reconnaissance plane. When I asked Dad about this, he said they had done their duty. I probed a bit more. Dad said after they arrived at the plane's wreckage, he realized they weren't just looking at a dead pilot. Yes, he was the enemy—but he was also someone's son, husband, and possibly father.

◀ *Mike, Gay, and Tony. Bronx Park, New York, August 1941.*

Maurice and Florence Provencher in Canada, 1943. ▶

Mom took two years off from her job at Ponemah during 1943-1944, though she carried on with the management of the Picard household.

In that period of time, an unexpected invitation from Mom's sister Florence and husband Maurice led to a visit with relatives in Canada. While there, my mother met her first cousins Raphael and Madeleine Gauthier. She corresponded with them for decades, until their deaths.

I was fortunate to meet Raphael and Madeleine in 1980 when they resided in New Iberia, Louisiana. A major energy company had hired me in 1979 to create a headquarters business library and to link the company's U.S. research libraries. The project required a business trip to New Orleans, the location of the company's offices supporting onshore/offshore oil exploration and production in the region. The weekend drive to New Iberia was just 4 hours each way.

Ice Hut No. 25 in Iceland, circa 1942. ▶

The Church had required Raphael to research his family history prior to becoming ordained. After I wrote to Madeleine in 1978, they provided me with nine generations of the Picard paternal line. With a single piece of paper, he removed a genealogy wall that had halted my research. The list revealed why my research had stalled: the original Picard surname was Destroismaisons dit Picard.

On December 16, 1943, just as Mom's favorite Marine was returning from Iceland, she and her brother Roger completed the naturalization process and took the oath of citizenship. Dad came home on furlough for two weeks before he reported to the Brooklyn Navy Yard to await his next assignment.

There were two things on Dad's mind: he would propose and then invite Gay to select an engagement ring. This reflected their lifelong pattern of making choices together. He also needed to see a dentist. The heavy mineral content in the Iceland water had pitted spots in his formerly perfect teeth. So, he experienced the first ten fillings of his life in a period of months after his return to the states.

Madeleine and Raphael Gauthier, 1980.

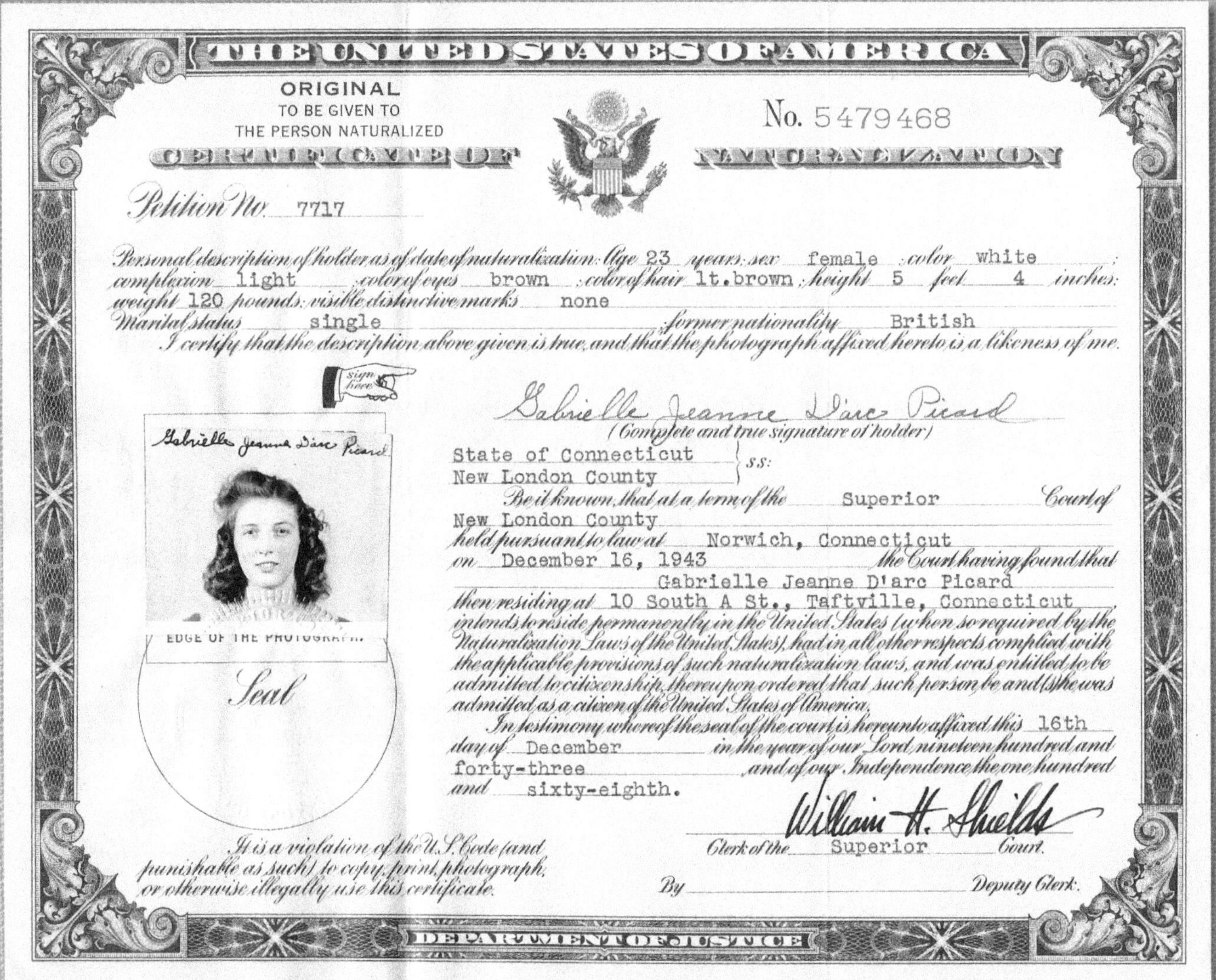

THE UNITED STATES OF AMERICA

ORIGINAL
TO BE GIVEN TO
THE PERSON NATURALIZED

No. 5479468

CERTIFICATE OF NATURALIZATION

Petition No. 7717

Personal description of holder as of date of naturalization: Age 23 years; sex female; color white; complexion light; color of eyes brown; color of hair lt.brown; height 5 feet 4 inches; weight 120 pounds; visible distinctive marks none

Marital status single; former nationality British

I certify that the description above given is true, and that the photograph affixed hereto is a likeness of me.

sign here

Gabrielle Jeanne D'arc Picard

(Complete and true signature of holder)

Gabrielle Jeanne D'arc Picard

EDGE OF THE PHOTOGRAPH

Seal

State of Connecticut }
New London County } ss:

Be it known, that at a term of the Superior Court of New London County held pursuant to law at Norwich, Connecticut on December 16, 1943 the Court having found that Gabrielle Jeanne D'arc Picard then residing at 10 South A St., Taftville, Connecticut intends to reside permanently in the United States (when so required by the Naturalization Laws of the United States), had in all other respects complied with the applicable provisions of such naturalization laws, and was entitled to be admitted to citizenship, thereupon ordered that such person be and (s)he was admitted as a citizen of the United States of America.

In testimony whereof the seal of the court is hereunto affixed this 16th day of December in the year of our Lord nineteen hundred and forty-three, and of our Independence the one hundred and sixty-eighth.

William H. Shields

Clerk of the Superior Court.

By _______________ Deputy Clerk.

It is a violation of the U.S. Code (and punishable as such) to copy, print, photograph, or otherwise illegally use this certificate.

DEPARTMENT OF JUSTICE

Gabrielle Picard becomes a citizen, 1943.

▲ *The U.S.S. LeJeune.*

By 1945, Mom had resumed working full time as a weaver at the Ponemah Mill, while still managing her father's household. From 1944-46, Dad was part of the Marine contingent that kept order on the *U.S.S. LeJeune*, a large Army troop transport vessel, based in Norfolk, Virginia.

Dad made more than thirty one-way trips across the Atlantic on this ship, departing mostly from New York, with destinations from Ireland to North Africa. President Franklin D. Roosevelt died in April 1945 while the *U.S.S. LeJeune* was en route from New York to Le Havre, France.

Aunt Vee, Dad's younger sister, has mentioned that she sometimes accompanied my mother to New York for visits with my father. In wartime, the trains between eastern Connecticut and Manhattan were packed. My mother and aunt usually sat on their suitcases the entire trip to New York City. In the evenings, night clubbing in Manhattan was the activity of choice, with the favorite spot being the Metropole.

Though the trains were bulging with commuters and travelers, my mother commented how strikingly

Ceremony aboard the U.S.S. LeJeune *after the death of Franklin D. Roosevelt.* ▼

Ellis, Vee, Gay, and Mike at the Metropole. ▼

Connie, Mary, Gay, Vee.

With Mike's sister Nelhe.

With Tony and Albina.

empty the streets of Manhattan were during the height of WWII. She said you would see women, children, and old men. The absence of young men on the streets of New York seemed eerie to Mom and something she would never forget, but she stressed that you still needed to pay attention!

My mother usually stayed at the Taft Hotel, well located and where she felt safe. On one visit to the city, though, my mother was walking down the street in mid-Manhattan, and realized a man was following her. She remained calm and continued to walk until she spotted a policeman. My mother said she pivoted, walked up to the stranger, and told him that if he didn't stop following her, she would report him. He high-tailed it quickly in another direction and didn't bother her again.

Most of us today can retell memorable stories we have heard from this historic period, but for those living it, World War II triggered a roller coaster of emotional reactions ranging from laughter and relief to fear and sadness—almost daily.

For couples in love and wanting to get married, the war seemed endless. My mother said they finally got tired of waiting: the separations were long and the reunions too short. When they could be together, they no longer wanted to spend precious time and money on traveling.

A Wartime Wedding in White

When they decided not to wait any longer for the end of the war, Dad requested a leave. Once granted, they set the date, and in a two-week whirlwind, Mom organized everything! Their mid-winter wedding in 1945 reflected their unique blend of practicality and finesse.

Even the dress had a story. Mom's brother Roger bought an exquisite dress in 1942 for his beautiful and beloved bride, Ada Rose Mainville, or as we knew her, Aunt Mickey. They graciously lent the dress to my mother, and later to Pauline Brouillette when she married Mom's youngest brother Jean Paul. Aunt Pauline told me recently the dress was very comfortable, and not altered for any of the three brides. You might say it was expertly designed for wartime schedules!

My parents' wedding announcement in the local newspaper described the dress and veil: "a princess styled gown of white brocaded satin with long train" and "tulle veil […] caught from a tiara of seeded pearls."

Not even a foot of snow mattered. Family and friends put on tire chains and drove my parents to get the marriage license, then to Taftville's Sacred Heart Church for the Monday wedding ceremony, and then to the wedding reception at the Silver

◀ *Gabrielle Picard and Sgt. Michael Janovicz marry. February 12, 1945.*

One dress - three beautiful brides!

▲ Roger Picard and Ada Rose Mainville marry, 1942. L-R: Floy Picard, Roger, Ada Rose, Rollie Picard, Joe Mainville, Doris Bazinet.

◀ Gabrielle Picard and Sgt. Michael Janovicz marry, 1945. L-R: Jean Paul Picard, Gabrielle Picard, Sgt. Michael Janovicz, Veronica Janovicz, 1945.

Jean Paul Picard and Pauline Brouillette marry, 1945. ▶

Dollar, a restaurant located about a mile south of the Ponemah Mill.

From the time of the wedding in mid-February 1945 until the Marines released Dad in June 1946, my parents just endured the weeks of separation between his leaves. They missed each other terribly and wrote mushy letters back and forth; at least that is how they seemed to my sister and me.

When we were little kids, the second level of our house was still unfinished and we would sometimes play upstairs. One day, my sister Cindy and I opened a large wooden chest, the size of a military footlocker. My dad had made it during WWII to hold his souvenirs from European and Mediterranean ports-of-call. We pawed through it, opening this and that. The chest was filled with my parents' treasured things, among them the stack of their wartime love letters.

Well, you should have seen my mother's face when we started to tease her about the letters. At first, Mom was grinning and squinting at us with that "you little rascals" look. Later, we got the lecture from the two of them about not going into other people's

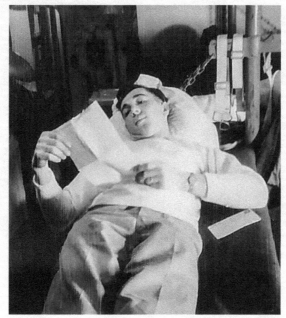

private things. We never saw the letters again; Mom probably burned them in the incinerator behind the house. In the end, it was our loss for being little brats.

I can only imagine the elation when each letter arrived. Mom did worry about her beloved Mike making it home. When looking back in later years, Dad would admit U-Boat torpedoes narrowly missed the ship a few times. Occasionally, the *U.S.S. LeJeune* had to cross the Atlantic without the protection of destroyers.

My mother would escape her fears and her taxing home life in two places. One was her first-shift weaving job at the Ponemah Mill. The other was the Hillcrest movie theatre, located just up the hill beyond Sacred Heart Church. How she looked forward to the weekly movies (and to reading movie star gossip magazines of the era). For pocket change, Mom could take in a double feature, see exciting coming attractions, and view a newsreel about WWII. My mother loved going to the movies, especially those featuring her favorite actors and actresses: Gary Cooper, Clark Gable, Robert Mitchum, Tyrone

WWII has ended finally. Her Mike will be released from service soon, 1946.

Power, Barbara Stanwyck, Myrna Loy, Deanna Durbin, Susan Hayward, and Jeanne Crain.

After she became engaged, Mom started to collect dishes. Movie theaters, during the 1930s and 1940s held "dish nights" when patrons could get a dish free or at a small price. Popular with moviegoers, the promotion increased movie attendance and theatre revenue while helping the female segment of their audience look to the future with hope.

Though not fine china, Mom felt these dishes were nice enough for the time when she and my father would get a place of their own. My mother collected two sets of dishes, one for everyday and one for special occasions.

The left photo shows a platter belonging to the everyday dish set. Despite the modest pedigree of the dishes, the scroll pattern you see around its edge was decorated in 23 carat gold.

The other set, the "good dishes," with their delicate pale pink flowers, now belong to Mom's granddaughter Diana.

New Beginnings

In 1944, the Marine Corp. asked if Dad would be willing to add two years onto his service. Dad agreed; it put him at risk longer, but he felt it was the right thing to do. Once the war ended, the Marine Corp. was able to release him a few months early, in June 1946.

Given the number of servicemen returning after WWII, apartments were scarce. The decision was that Dad would live with Mom's family in Taftville for a while. It would be convenient for both of them to get to their jobs.

Well, some plans change quickly! One night at dinner there was a scene. My aunt Rollie, also sitting at the supper table, said everything happened so fast. Floy, my mother's sister, threw a hot cup of coffee in my father's face. (No one, past or present, could seem to recall what triggered the unkind act.)

According to both my mother and Aunt Rollie, my father stood up and said, "Gay, get your things. We're going to my mother's." They left soon after. Aside from feeling terrible about the hot coffee hitting my

◀ *Mike, Gay, cousin Connie, Uncle Tony.*

Gay with a calf near the barn, circa 1946. ▶

dad, the only regret my mother would mention about this moment was that she had very little time to collect a few sentimental things. She grabbed her clothes and her mother's cut glass celery server.

It is possible my father sensed before the incident that he might need a contingency plan for where they would reside. Anyone who knew my father would tell you he would not start an argument in my mother's home, but he would defend my mother, if others were not being reasonable.

For a second time, Mom's sister Floy had indirectly improved my mother's life, though my father suffered momentarily. This incident finally freed my mother from her second full time job.

At the farmhouse in Norwichtown, her mother-in-law, Mary, appreciated my mother's assistance, her pleasant personality, and her willingness to learn things about the farm. During her years living at the farmhouse, Mom mastered the preparation of Eastern European foods, such as pierogi and golabki, as well as fried chicken, a specialty of my Lithuanian grandmother. Our family would clamor for these dishes throughout the years ahead. I confess that, even after making them with her twice, I still cannot replicate my mother's delicious golabki!

Mom noticed that everyone helped with chores on the farm, but there seemed to be energy left to enjoy life more. Mom adored all the fresh food, from vegetables to eggs, milk, and cheese, and especially the clear, delicious well water. She even learned how to use a rifle, and a bow and arrow.

Within nine months of my father's return from WWII service, Dad's father gifted him a land parcel next to the farmhouse. At the moment my father filed the building permit on March 29, 1947 you might say the two of them became a human loom. Mom's pay from her Ponemah weaving job became the warp and Dad's labor became the weft of their dream to build a mortgage free house of their own.

While building the house, they continued to reside in the farmhouse with his family and live on Dad's apprentice carpenter income. As my father learned the basics of carpentry and construction with Duff Construction, he often applied the techniques right away.

House construction: Norwichtown, 1947-1950.

Years later when I noticed the basement of my parent's house was made of cinder blocks rather than poured concrete, I asked my uncle Tony why my dad had made that choice. He laughed as he explained, "Mike would rather have used concrete, but he hadn't learned yet how to do that! He wanted to move forward."

My mother's beloved Mike (on the ladder) worked weekends and nights with his brother Tony (at the sawhorse) often assisting. In the same period of time (1947-1950), the two men also built a house diagonally across the street for Aunt Albina and Uncle Tony. Originally, the plan was to finish Mike and Gay's house first, but when Aunt Albina discovered she was expecting, Mike and Tony reversed the sequence. My cousin Paul should feel great about that change on his behalf!

My father kept a detailed log of every out-of-pocket expense. (The roster does not include expenses for the second story, finished in the 1970s.)

Here is a sample page from his log.

This is a breakdown of the total out-of-pocket construction expenses incurred 1947-1950.

EXPENSE CATEGORY	AMOUNT
Foundation, Cement, Sand, & Concrete	677.37
Framing	1254.46
Sheathing	658.29
Outside Siding, Trim, Windows, & Doors	1457.41
Roofing, Bdlg Paper, Flashing, Guttering, etc.	333.23
Paint, Varnish, Brushes, Caulking, etc.	141.61
Nails	177.79
Plumbing & Heating	1633.99
Water Supply, Drainage, & Sewerage	856.25
Wiring & Electrical Fixtures	252.18
Insulation, Lath, Grounds	258.72
Plaster, Floor Sanding, Tilework, Linoleum, Rubber Tile, Counter Top	930.34
Inside Trim, Floring, Doors, Cabinets, etc	784.46
Outside Hardware	23.46
Inside Hardware	77.82
Grading, Landscaping, Lawns	82.40
Miscellaneous	64.50
Tools, Equipment, etc.	678.08
TOTAL	**$10,342.36**

I think Dad compiled the expenses as much for my mother's pleasure as for his own factual interest.

In March 1950, Gabrielle and Michael Janovicz settled into their new mortgage free home and awaited the birth of their first daughter. ■

Part Two

Return to Taftville and the Ponemah Mill

The Ponemah Mill, Building No. 1 (the Main Building), October 2014.

T here is nothing like a giant artifact, in this case a famous mill and its village, to rouse one's curiosity about times past. I guess you could say my family history is tethered to the Ponemah Mill. At least ten of the fifteen members of my mother's immediate family worked at this storied fabric mill during their lifetimes.

For those who hold the Ponemah Mill and its history dear, our "great hope" is that the strong, majestic main building will live on in a purposeful new life. I am optimistic about the residential conversion occurring as this book goes to print, but a bit sad that descendants of Taftville families will be unable soon to see what I and others viewed in 2014.

As a family historian, I am thankful that the current owners have permitted numerous tours of the interior space of Ponemah's Main Building. Hopefully, the photos taken during the walking tours will provide visual answers for those trying to imagine how things once looked.

Since the 1990s, WALKTOBER has offered a fabulous series of walking tours and events in eastern Connecticut. WALKTOBER has featured a Ponemah Mill walk numerous times.

Sponsored by The Last Green Valley organization, WALKTOBER has grown, thanks to the enthusiastic support of area residents. The 2017 schedule ran from September 23-November 4, and included all sorts of historical and cultural subjects, as well as activities during which you can appreciate the natural beauty of eastern Connecticut and Massachusetts.

It has been my privilege to attend two WALKTOBER tours of the Ponemah Mill, the first in 2004, and the second in 2014. They both opened doorways to deeper understanding about my mother and her life, especially in the Ponemah years.

TAFTVILLE c. 1940

1. No. 1 Mill 2. No. 2 Mill 3. No. 3 Mill 4. Maintenance Departments 5. Canal and Water Wheel 6. Boarding House 7. Company Store and Ponemah Hall 8. Congregational Church 9. Providence St. 10. South A St. 11. South B St. 12. South C St. 13. North A St. 14. North B St. 15. Second Ave. a.k.a. Front St. 16. Third Ave. 17. Slater Ave. (foremen's residences) 18. Superintendent's Mansion 19. Wequonnoc School 20. Sacred Heart Church 21. Sacred Heart School 22. Dugas Studio (Est. 1882, contains a photographic history of Taftville) 23. ShymaShyla Club (site of first Sacred Heart Church) 24. Site of first Sacred Heart School (Nuns' Residence is still evident.) 25. Caron Residence on a high ledge 26. Providence Street "Ball Ground" 27. Site of Balancing Rock 28. Cow Barn 29. Horse barn 30. Site of Prentice Roller Shop. Below: The Number 4 Weave Shop, built in 1910, was the largest building in Norwich, 700 feet long and 200 feet wide. Not shown herein are the New Village and Terrace Ave. buildings which consisted of 148 apartments in 36 buildings.

Walktober Ponemah Mill Tour - 2004

In 2004, when my sister Cindy first alerted me about the WALKTOBER Ponemah Mill tour, I telephoned the Last Green Valley office to inquire about just how rigorous this particular walk was, explaining that my mother was mobile, but 84 years old. The woman chuckled and said, "I think she'll be fine. The tour guide, Rene Dugas, is 90-something!"

Three generations of the Dugas family's photography studio captured life in Taftville during the hundred years of the Ponemah Mill era. Rene leveraged the family's photo collection further, by authoring several pictorial books about the village, its residents, and the times.

Rene began the tour at the Taftville Knights of Columbus Hall where he circulated a stack of photos. Even though half a century had passed since she lived there, Mom studied every photo. She kept turning towards me and smiling as she repeatedly pointed to faces she recognized.

Rene Dugas surely had a presence. Of wiry body and nimble step, he exhibited more energy than many people half his age—and a bit of drama, too. At one point during the tour, he raised his arms and exclaimed that "everybody knew everybody" in Taftville.

On that clear, sunny fall day in 2004, Mom and I walked the Taftville streets and then around the Mill's exterior, while Rene lent his unique blend of history and humor about life in the village where almost all the residents worked for Ponemah. He noted that the Mill was always hiring. Rene joked that he had been fired and rehired numerous times.

My mother posed in front of the bell tower of Ponemah Mill's Building No. 1, also called the Main Building, where she had worked on the fourth floor as a weaver sixty years earlier.

The former residence of the Picard family on South A Street, Taftville. ▶

◀ *Gabrielle Picard Janovicz, in front of the Ponemah Mill's Main Building, 2004.*

Mom reminisced that you could hear the Ponemah bell from anywhere in Taftville. She explained its first ringing each day occurred about 5:00 a.m. I asked her if you could sleep through the bell ringing. Mom burst out laughing and replied, "It could jolt you right out of bed, if you weren't already up!" Mom remembered a second ringing about 10-15 minutes before her shift started. If you weren't already walking towards the Mill, the melodious suggestion was to "put a wiggle" in it. The final ring at 6:00 a.m. signaled the startup of machines and beginning of her shift.

Mom and I turned off the walking tour briefly onto South A Street. Right away, she spotted the house where she grew up, despite its updated appearance. (See photo previous page.) In Mom's youth, the village consisted of neat, look-alike white houses, built by the Mill's owners to house their work force.

The Picard family of fifteen rented the four-bedroom apartment on the right side of this duplex. When my sister Cindy and I were kids, we complained repeatedly about having to share a double bed. My mother would remind us that she and her siblings slept four to a bed when she was young! Her statement would start sternly, but then we'd see a grin sneaking out and finally she couldn't help laughing.

Walktober Ponemah Mill Tour - 2014

That image of four little kids lined up in a double bed brought a smile to my heart as I arrived in Taftville for my second tour—now ten years later. When I learned that the WALKTOBER tour on Sunday, October 26, 2014 would include the *inside* of the Mill, I immediately decided to go.

▲ *Departing the Taftville Fire Station, 2014.*

I still regret that Mom and I could not experience this together. My mother had died in January 2009, rather suddenly from pneumonia, while in the long goodbye of Alzheimer's. Knowing that the Ponemah Mill was in the process of being converted into residential space, I felt it might be the last opportunity for me to walk in my mother's footsteps.

A good-sized crowd was assembling at the Taftville Fire Station. While we waited for the tour to begin, a slideshow ran inside the firehouse, with a wide array of images representing Taftville's history.

▼ *Intersection of Providence Street and North 3rd Avenue, 2014.*

The remains of Sacred Heart Church, Taftville, after the 1956 fire. ▶

Fire Chief Tim Jencks gave an introduction and then we went outside and headed down Providence Street toward the Ponemah Mill.

While pausing at North 3rd Avenue, Fire Chief Jencks provided some village history, including selected events from Taftville's fire protection and incident history.

I was not aware of the disastrous 1915 fire in the village, nor the one at the Sacred Heart Convent School in 1927. My mother was born in 1920, so the latter fire event may be the reason my mother started school at second grade level, rather than first.

Anyone who reads about Taftville's first one hundred years will conclude that two hearts united the body of people in this tightly knit community—one at each end of Providence Street, the main street of the village. One was the Ponemah Mill. The other was Sacred Heart Church.

So, when a major fire broke out inside the Church during an early Sunday Mass in April 1956 and destroyed the building, the community was devastated.

The firefighters did not want to break the beautiful stained glass windows, so they were somewhat constrained in battling this fire. The photo above, with a view from the rear of the Church, displays the extensive damage.

For several months, while the Church was being rebuilt, the Ponemah Mill hosted Sunday Mass on the second floor of its Building No. 3. Some of my cousins might be in this Mass at Ponemah photo on the next page. Uncle Jean Paul, Aunt Pauline, and their growing family lived right on Providence Street. My aunt told me recently that my cousin Susie made her First Communion at Ponemah during this time.

◀ *The major fire at Sacred Heart Church, Taftville, April 1956.*

The author, standing next to the display of her 2014 blog article in the history exhibit of the Taftville 150-Year Celebration.

*T*he Taftville Fire Department spearheaded Taftville's 150-year celebration, held July 30-August 2, 2015. The event's planning team invited me to display the blog article I wrote following the 2014 WALKTOBER tour of Ponemah (and the basis for this book). So, I spent a good part of Saturday there, in the event's fascinating historical exhibit. A steady stream of people strolled through and I enjoyed many wonderful conversations with attendees and with other exhibitors, most of whom had heritage ties, like me, to Taftville.

While at that Taftville 150 celebration, I admired an antique fire vehicle on display and talked with one of the Taftville firefighters about it.

In the 1930s, the Ponemah Fire Company No. 1 disbanded and the Taftville Hose Company No. 2 assumed responsibility for the entire village. At that time, the Ponemah unit donated the truck they had been using: a 1910 Cadillac touring car that had been converted to a fire truck. At one time it had belonged to the Mill's treasurer. This is that truck!

The 1910 Fire Truck of Ponemah Fire Company No. 1 .

▲ *Ponemah Mill hosted Sunday Mass.*

Ironically, I have a happy memory associated with the aftermath of the fire. My dad was part of the construction crew that rebuilt this church where my parents were married in 1945.

When I was growing up, we often visited the Picard cousins who lived on Providence St. So, during one visit in the summertime, my cousin Susie and I walked up the street to see the repair activity and say hello to my dad.

We stood across the street on the sidewalk, but couldn't see him at all. So, we yelled and yelled until my father came to the edge of the building, near the top. All the men were smiling down at us, two little kids five and six at the time, carrying on a loud conversation with my dad. That memory still plays like a film in my mind.

With our Picard cousins, circa 1959. Back: Bernice, Cindy, Susie, Richard, Leo. Front: Norman, Donna, Betty Lou. ▶

While our WALKTOBER Tour group paused at the intersection of North 3rd Avenue and Providence Street, Fire Chief Jencks pointed out that if you look northerly up North 3rd Avenue, the same view as this photo, and veer right at the end of the street, you would arrive at the location where Ponemah's executives used to reside.

The proximity was convenient for their work and near the Taftville Congregational Church, the "green church" across from the northwest corner of Ponemah Building No. 1. Ponemah donated the land and the green paint to the Church's founders.

Our walking tour continued down Providence Street and stopped at this Ponemah building, right, which housed the medical office for the Mill. Fire Chief Tim Jencks told our 2014 tour group that the Ponemah Mill provided free medical services to its employees. If a medical problem could not be handled in the Taftville medical office, the employee was sent to Backus Hospital where Ponemah paid for two beds.

This Ponemah building housed the medical office. ▶

Located at the base of Providence Street, this building, below, was directly across from another Ponemah building that housed a meat market and grocery store, as well as other shops and small businesses. Both buildings sat directly across CT Route 97 from Ponemah's Main Building.

* * *

My mother worked the first shift at Ponemah. In mid-afternoon on her short walk home (about two blocks) she often stopped to pick up food items for the family's evening meal. Undoubtedly, my organized mother was already thinking about the household chores she would manage well into the evening.

My grandfather expected a fresh soup before their supper "every evening" Mom once told me. She described the typical scene most days in their household. The men in the family returned home from their jobs, sat down, and relaxed with a smoke or tobacco chew while they waited for dinner to be ready. After dinner Mom's brothers often went out. Once a week,

◀ Ralph Picard, circa 1938.

Gabrielle Picard, 1943. ▶

either my grandfather or my mother's brother Ralph would wash the linoleum floors.

The female members of the household bustled about completing the myriad of housekeeping chores waiting for them before and after the evening meal. When my mother was a child, food was cooked in large pots, the laundry was washed by hand, and piles of clean clothing and bed sheets needed to be ironed. As more of the females became adults and departed the household, the family began to use the services of a nearby Chinese laundry, but the chore list every day was still substantial. Vital statistics would later reveal that, collectively, my mother and her sisters outlived their brothers—by an average of fifteen years.

At times during the years I was growing up, my mother would shake her head, as if in disbelief, while saying she "put in 8 hours at the Mill and then another 8 hours at home" most days. She always felt gratitude, though, towards her older sister, Florence, who had shown compassion to the younger children in the 1930s. Rather than shifting the load off her own adult shoulders, Aunt Florence gradually introduced my mother and the younger girls to housework, trying to let them enjoy some of their childhood.

Even so, by her early twenties in 1943, my exhausted mother requested two weeks off from her boss at the Ponemah Mill. When she returned two *years* later, her boss was speechless at first, and then exclaimed, "Where have you been, Gabi?"

I believe this exhaustion break was not just my mother's story; other young women in the Taftville of that time must have experienced what my mother did. After all, she was working the equivalent of two full time jobs. My mother told me her typical day ended at 11:00 P.M. and began again at 5:00 A.M. Sometimes she felt like she had just closed her eyes.

Mom spoke to us often about the value of "paying attention" in one's life. She understood the impacts of her mother's premature death on their large family, and of course, on herself. During my childhood, when the subject of health came up, my mother would say to us, "I take care of myself, because otherwise I wouldn't be able to take care of you." She drank lots of milk and well water, and ate conservatively—avoiding candy, soda, and other sweetened products long before it was fashionable, while also keeping them away from us because they would "rot our teeth." My mother was quite proud that she retained her teeth through her lifetime. I think she would be pleased that I am sharing this fact, as I know it meant a lot to her!

▲ *Cindy, Bernice, and baby Donna, 1958.*

I can recall my mother becoming seriously ill only once when my sisters and I were young. She experienced a painful bursitis attack in the 1960s, one of the few times in my young life that I saw my mother bedridden for days and crying from the pain.

Mom didn't need to ask Dad for help. He immediately pitched in, doing the cooking and keeping the house in order while she was incapacitated. None of us were surprised. Dad was always helping someone.

Mom's whole face would smile when she told the story of how each time she went into the hospital to deliver one of us, she returned to sparkling floors. Dad had cleaned and waxed every floor in the house to welcome her and the new baby home.

WALKTOBER tour group approaching the "front door" of the Ponemah Mill, October 2014. ▶

My mother felt fortunate to have married a wonderful man. She would note also that her bosses at the Ponemah Mill were "great to her." She once told me the story of her boss bringing her a section of fabric she had produced, and asking what she saw. A weaver only a short time, she was unsure what he really wanted to know, so she didn't respond immediately, waiting for more of a clue. He then patiently asked if the fabric looked okay to her. She said, "Yes, it does."

Well—her boss arranged to have her eyes tested! It wasn't long before she was wearing glasses and could see the imperfections she needed to spot.

* * *

Our 2014 WALKTOBER group continued to the "front door" of the Ponemah Mill complex: the intersection of Providence Street (CT Route 169) and Norwich Avenue (CT Route 97).

Known as the Main Building, or Building No. 1, it was built from 1867-1871, during the first wave of development of the 600-acre tract of farmland adjacent to the Shetucket River.

I thought it was great that the Taftville Fire Department, largely volunteer, escorted our group

The courtyard behind Building No. 1.

The "L" is ahead in the distance.

The administration building is to the right, beyond the photo edge. ▶

and ensured safe walking conditions here and later in the Mill. The south tower on the right, closest to the fire vehicle, still holds the famous Ponemah Mill bell. Fire Chief Tim Jencks told our walking tour group that Hurricane Sandy damaged this tower in 2012.

This Main Building contained more than 50,000 panes of glass and countless bricks. The Ponemah Mill bricks were sourced from Dayville, Connecticut, a town near Danielson in the northeast corner of the state. They were transported via railroad the twenty miles to Taftville during mill construction from 1867-71.

The name Ponemah, derived from a Native American word, is sometimes translated as "afterwards" or "afterlife" or "our future hope." The last phrase seems most frequently associated with the Ponemah Mill, perhaps because the letters for the word "hope" are embedded.

Our 2014 tour group was now standing in the courtyard behind Ponemah Building No. 1, the Main Building. Onekey, LLC, a construction firm based in New Jersey, is renovating these Ponemah structures. Fire Chief Jencks noted that virtually every reconstruction aspect must pass through the historical commission.

The main weave shops were housed on the fourth and fifth floors of Building No. 1. (The fifth floor has dormer windows.) Note the original fire escapes, their ladders removed, and the tower extension that contained the restrooms.

Located between the Main Building (left) and the administration building, the "L" was part of the vertical corridor in which the plunging force of the river

▲ *Above the power generation area in the "L."*

▲ *A train track extension brought train cars close to the Ponemah buildings.*

water was transformed into electricity—two floors beneath the floor where our group stood.

The operation is easier to imagine if you look at this photo below taken when we walked behind the Mill. This photo shows the water intake side of the "L."

The courtyard behind Building No. 1 held a circular train track extension. Incoming raw materials and outgoing fabric products were loaded for transport.

This photo above shows a train car at the rear of Ponemah Building No. 2, which was adjacent and just south of the Main Building. You can see how closely the train cars nestled into the buildings.

Fire Chief Jencks next led us into the Mill's executive and administrative offices, a single-story building located to the right of the "L" in the courtyard (photo on previous page), but not quite visible.

The water intake area at Ponemah Mill. ▼

Inside Ponemah's administration building. ▼

travel back in time and see and hear the Ponemah Mill in its heyday!

***

The final segment of the WALKTOBER tour took us into Ponemah Building No. 1, the large Main Building where my mother worked during the period 1937 to 1950.

Remember the two towers that you could see in the front view of the main building? The towers housed the staircases, accessible from front and rear entrances. Their architectural design, positioned external to the building, ensured maximum floor space on every level. This external tower design was also applied to the restrooms.

As we entered the building through the south tower doors, the tension of anticipation began to release from my body. My curiosity was surging.

Immense space existed in this Ponemah Building No. 1, as we soon discovered. The building measures about 775 X 85 feet (the outside dimensions are not consistent across sources), and has long been cleared of the mill materials, equipment, and furniture my mother saw in her workdays.

All sorts of preliminary product activities occurred on the first three floors of the Main Building, from carding the cotton, to spinning the thread, to filling the bobbins for the army of looms upstairs.

When I stepped away from the group towards the large windows on the east side of this administration building, my reward was this panoramic view of the fall foliage along the Shetucket River. From the windows, one could easily see the railroad tracks and the close proximity to the river—the source of electricity for the mill's operations.

Haven't the interior renovations brought back the beauty of this grand old building? I truly wish I could

◀ *Interior renovations in the administration building.*

▲ *Original flooring in the Mill.*

▲ *The south tower staircase of the Main Bldg.*

▲ *Third floor, Ponemah Building No. 1.*

Three of my mother's brothers worked in these types of mill activities. Leonard worked as a carder, Conrad as a doffer, and Ralph as a spinner. A carder, operating by hand or aided by machinery, disentangled clumps in the cotton, washed the fibers, and aligned the individual cotton fibers in parallel to each other in preparation for spinning the thread. A doffer removed the bobbins wound with cotton thread and replaced them with empty ones.

The firm converting the Mill left a section of original flooring intact on the first floor. Many generations of Taftville residents walked across these wooden boards located just inside the south tower's rear entrance.

It was time…to climb the stairs of Building No. 1. Close your eyes. Can you hear the thunder of the employee traffic these twin staircases carried at the start and end of each shift? Many of us climbing the stairs

during this tour were retracing the everyday footsteps of our parents, grandparents, aunts and uncles.

Here's a look at the columns typical of the first three floors. This photo (top right) was taken on the third floor of Ponemah Mill's Building No. 1, along with this shot below which represents one of the most interesting things I learned on this walking tour.

Notice the construction groove where the support beam rests. Fire Chief Tim Jencks mentioned that the owners of the Mill understood they had reduced the risk of fire in this mill by constructing it largely of brick. They also knew the wood in the ceiling supports, floors, staircases, and trim, as well as the raw materials and finished fabric would feed any fire that got started.

So, if ever the Mill suffered damage by fire, the owners expected this groove design would facilitate quick

◀ *The Ponemah Mill's ceiling groove design.*

▲ *Staircase to the fourth floor of Building No. 1.*

▲ *South tower door to the fourth floor, Building No. 1.*

replacement of all the main support beams, originally hewn from giant Canadian timber.

We were now climbing the stairs to the fourth floor, where my mother worked as a weaver.

I held back at first...and then passed through the 4th floor doorway, a wave of exhilaration coursing through me.

Once inside, I looked right and left — and then right and left again.

Though substantial, my first impression of the space was that it was smaller than I expected. It didn't seem to match the imposing size and presence of the building's exterior.

Main Building 4th floor looking LEFT (southerly) from the south tower entry.▼

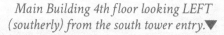

Main Building 4th floor looking RIGHT (northerly) from the south tower entry.▼

Aunt Rollie, circa 1950. ▶

For a few moments, I considered that maybe we were not viewing the full length of the building; maybe one of the ends was blocked off. After a few minutes of walking the floor periphery and locating the two towers, I realized this was, indeed, the entire fourth floor of Ponemah Building No. 1.

I had questions, so, a few days after the Ponemah walking tour I telephoned Aunt Rollie to learn what she could recall from her 1940s work experience. Recently, we revisited this subject in another delightful conversation about looms, batteries and shuttles.

My Aunt Rollie, five years younger than my mother, was employed by Ponemah, too. She went to work there in 1942, starting as a battery hand, just as my mother had done years earlier.

Battery hands did lots of running, wheeling carts of the refilled giant bobbins to the weaving floors over and over during their work shift—and quickly, as the electrified looms would stop if the battery emptied of bobbins. Aunt Rollie recalled that each battery held about 15-20 bobbins.

The battery hands wheeled their cart along the "alleyways," between (the boundary of) two weaver's looms. If time permitted, they stopped to reload the batteries of each loom. If other areas needed refills more, they left a supply of fresh bobbins for the weaver to load as needed.

Though appearing to be a circular wheel, Aunt Rollie emphasized that the battery of each loom did not move. The shuttle flew back and forth horizontally, carrying (the weft) thread between the vertical (warp) threads, which the loom raised and unraised in a pre-determined pattern, according to the weave specifications for the fabric.

When the shuttle depleted the thread of the bobbin it was carrying, it ejected the spent bobbin and loaded a fresh one from the battery. During the process a very fine knot was tied automatically to join the thread ends of the spent and replacement bobbins. Aunt Rollie said the weaver would hear a click, and shortly the shuttle would resume its high-speed path back and forth.

The first U.S. mill to import Egyptian cotton, Ponemah gained its competitive edge by being the first to manufacture fine fabrics of the type previously imported from England. The fine gauge "higher number" threads were woven to produce this high-quality fabric, coveted in the marketplace.

▲ *Draper Northrop Loom.*

Close-up of a Bobbin Battery. ▶

The Draper Northrop automatic loom and battery with self-threading shuttle revolutionized the weaving process, beginning in the late 1800s, allowing weavers to manage many more looms at once.

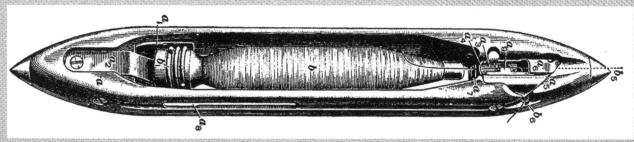

▲ *A Draper loom shuttle.*

Aunt Rollie explained that the weaving floors were kept warm. From pipes that lined the ceiling, sprinklers cast steam over the Draper looms, "like a mist," my aunt whispered to me. (See the mist in the photo at right.) The fine gauge cotton thread needed to be damp while the looms were weaving the fabric, otherwise the thread would break—not a good thing!

Weavers stood throughout their shift, moving from loom to loom in the group they managed. Periodically, they would check the fabric for any visible thread ends. When they spied such a spot, they would maneuver a small weaving hook to pull the thread through, and then tie a tiny knot and clip the end(s). All evidence of the errant thread(s) would disappear, as if a gentle wave had rolled in and smoothed the sand.

Generally, weavers produced a plain off-white color fabric. Ponemah's customers finished the fabrics further if their business required, adding color via dye or printing the surface. For years, my mother tapped into her supply of damaged mill fabric, of varying weights, using it periodically for items such as our quilt covers and the laundry bag I took to my college dorm. Aunt Rollie didn't recall that the Mill sold discounted damaged fabric to its employees. She believed my mother's boss gave it to her, because my mother ruined so little fabric.

As often is true with equipment, things do go awry at times. When their loom areas sat next to one another, Aunt Rollie recalls moments when my mother could tell that one of my aunt's looms was misbehaving. Mom would walk over to see if she could assist. More experienced, my mother sometimes reassured my aunt, "Oh, just do this, and I think it will be okay." Or, her facial expression would convey that my aunt needed to request help.

When I visited the Windham Mill Museum, the director told me the high-speed shuttle would break loose occasionally and fly out into the workspace. It might land on the open floor. On occasion, though, it would hit and injure a person or damage a loom nearby.

I asked my aunt about this and she confirmed shuttles broke loose now and then. Loom fixers in fabric mills remedied all kinds of loom malfunctions, but at Ponemah they had a special name for employees who were particularly adept at fixing the damage to fabric, warp threads, and the set-up at a loom damaged by an airborne shuttle. They called this person a "smash piecer." A scarce talent, they more typically worked the first shift, and often were weavers.

The operational records of the Quinebaug and Wauregan, sister mills in the northeast corner of

Connecticut, indicate these mills designated a job category and pay rate for "smash piecer." The 1943 weekly rate at that time for Weavers was $25.38, for Smash Piecers $29.00, for Loom Fixers $37.26, and for Battery Hands $20.00.

**

Somewhere on this 4th floor of Building No. 1 my mother managed twelve looms. It was so quiet now. I closed my eyes, trying to imagine the sea of looms that once clattered in this space.

Aunt Rollie said my mother's looms were located right outside the office of Mom's boss, Mr. McKeon. My aunt explained that Jimmy McKeon liked being able to check on my mother easily. Mom was a high-volume producer with a low defect rate. Mr. McKeon wanted to keep her looms humming.

In checking the 1940 U.S. Census data, I found an entry for James J. McKeon, who was an assistant foreman at a cotton textile mill. He was forty years old and lived on Occum Road with his wife, Alice, and sons Robert, Roland, and Gerald.

Robert "Red" McKeon, one of his sons, would become a legend in firefighting during his 34 years of service as the Occum Fire Chief. He advanced numerous firefighting protocols, including the integration of Emergency Medical Services (EMS), considered routine today. As an example, my firefighter nephew Stephen became EMS certified while he served as a volunteer in the small eastern Connecticut town where he grew up—about five years before he became a professional firefighter.

James J. McKeon: Mom's boss. ▶

My mother's boss, James J. McKeon, also known as Jim or Jimmy, began his career as a loom fixer, but was a house painter in 1930 according to the Federal Census data. The Great Depression had hit the mills hard. In the mid-1930s, his father, John J. McKeon, began an assignment with the Ponemah Mill, one of many mills owned by his employer.

The Mill's owners had requested a reduction in its tax assessment in 1932. The Norwich Superior Court had refused to grant the request. Ponemah's owners planned to move the operations out of Norwich. A public meeting attended by five thousand people convinced the owners they should try harder to find a solution to the financial challenges they were facing. Ultimately, they sold the houses in Ponemah's mill village, to mostly their employees, and in doing so, greatly reduced their tax assessment.

A company man, John J. McKeon (the father of my mother's boss) went wherever the mill owners needed him. Both of his sons and their families would move with him. The families were located at mill sites in North Grosvenordale, Connecticut and Utica, New York prior to Taftville. At Ponemah, his son James J. (Mom's boss) served as an Assistant Foreman and son John, a loom fixer.

▲ Sisters Rollie and Gay reminisce, 1985.

▲ Aunt Rollie's children, John and Jeanne, circa 1956.

Until a conversation in 2014, I didn't know that Aunt Rollie also became a weaver. An expression of surprise must have betrayed me because the first thing she added, nodding her head with authority, was, "Yes, I was a weaver, too. But, your mother—she was an expert."

At that moment, it was as if a window opened into my mother's life. Tears began to well up in my eyes. I could envision my mother standing confidently at her looms.

My mother's "essence" has become clearer from hearing Aunt Rollie's recollections. Our family enjoyed many visits with Aunt Rollie and her family when I was a child. I am grateful for our lively chats and her amazing memories.

Beyond the joyful nature of these conversations with Aunt Rollie and other relatives, I continue to be fascinated by the endless nature of the memory reservoir, much like the hidden spring deep beneath my parents' 33-foot well in Norwichtown that never ran dry. Tapping one person's reservoir opens a stream of memories and images in both people, and sometimes with other relatives, in conversations days, weeks, months, or years later.

Had I asked more questions in the 1970s when I first interviewed my mother's siblings, I would have learned even more about the family, Ponemah, and weaving from my aunts Ida, Florence, and Rita, as well as my uncle Paul. All were weavers at Ponemah.

I do recall a particular visit with my parents in the 1990s when I got a glimpse of my mother's weaving finesse. I wanted to use my mother's sewing machine to repair a garment. All her bobbins contained thread. Neither of the two with the closest color match contained enough thread for my repair.

My mother became quiet. I watched her cross the two ends of the bobbins' threads on her index finger. Then, in a quick, circular swishing motion with her thumb pressed against that thread cross sitting on her index finger, she created the tiniest knot I have ever seen. She looked at it and laughed, then exclaimed, "I am amazed I could still do that." We spooled the thread of one bobbin over the other. While making my sewing repair, I must say I was curious, so I manually moved the stitching wheel slowly. The tiny knot (the weaver's knot my mother had mastered more than forty years earlier) passed right through the eye of the sewing machine's needle!

So, standing on the fourth floor of Ponemah, I was looking around and wondering. Where exactly had my mother's looms been located?

Aunt Rollie said that Mr. McKeon's office did not have walls, and she remembered recently that it had a glass barrier. I suspect his office space was sparsely furnished, consisting perhaps of a desk, a couple chairs, and a few other essentials.

At first, I thought his office might have been located on the fourth-floor landing. It was a

well-lighted space and I had seen an office roughed in on the staircase landing of another Ponemah floor.

But, in a more recent conversation, Aunt Rollie remembered that Mr. McKeon's office was located in a corner of the 4th floor. My mother's looms were next to his office, and my aunt's looms were next to my mother's.

My mother's loom area, then, may have stood between the south tower doors (shown above) and one of the south corners of the 4th floor.

▼ *Main Building 4th floor landing.*

Or her looms were located near the north side corners of the floor (see previous photo).

Well, one thing is clear from my journey back to Ponemah and Taftville. The main responsibility of the bosses, the weavers, the loom fixers, the carders, the spinners, the doffers, the battery hands, and virtually all the jobs at Ponemah was to keep the looms running. So, as my mother and Aunt Rollie conveyed, all weavers needed to pay attention constantly to their looms. Any trip to the bathroom would be a quick one, if you were a weaver.

Perhaps the mill design embedded that message as well in the minds of employees. I am unsure how many employees worked on each floor of Ponemah Building No. 1 during the years my mother worked there, but the small size of the bathrooms surprised me at first. Once I reframed the fourth floor in my mind into clusters of looms, each assigned to a single weaver, it helped me to adjust my first impression.

▲ *The bathroom's sink area.*

Each floor contained two bathrooms for men and two for women. This bathroom entrance (photo below left) is directly across from the 4th floor south tower entry staircase we used during the 2014 tour.

The bathrooms for men and women seemed identical in size and design. The respective entries were open design, with an arch instead of a door, like facilities common in our airports today.

As soon as you passed under the entry arch, you were in this chamber (above). Since it was visible from the work floor, this space probably housed the sinks.

Based on a favorite story my mother liked to tell, I suspect a portable screen may have stood in front of the entrance to each bathroom. Mom remembered an instance when she was about to enter the bathroom. A male boss called out her name. He asked her to check if a particular female employee was in the bathroom,

◀ *Bathroom entrance.*

▲ The bathroom's toilet area.

▲ The fifth floor of Building No. 1.

and if inside, to tell this woman that he said she needed to get back to her job. My mother nodded, walked into the bathroom, and sure enough, the woman was bending over the sink, washing her hair! Mom said she conveyed the message.

Within the right side wall of the sink area is another archway, not visible in the photo. It leads to an inner chamber, shown above.

Since this inner chamber was not visible from the initial floor entry, this area likely contained the toilets.

How many toilets do you guess this contained?

Notice that the stucco-like white finish has fallen away near the window, and may not be original to the building.

***

I hated to leave the fourth floor, but there was one more floor to see in Ponemah's Main Building—the fifth floor where the finest fabrics were woven.

The fifth-floor struts and slender steel rods (bolted downward through the fourth-floor ceiling) support *both* the fifth and fourth floors. The design eliminated the need for ceiling to floor columns—which opened the floor space to more looms and easier placement.

The last tour stop inside the building was the fifth-floor landing, right below the cupola that holds the famous Ponemah Bell.

◀ The Ponemah Bell.

The three giant windows that grace the 5th floor landing in Building No. 1.

While light poured in from the three giant circular windows gracing the fifth-floor landing, Fire Chief Jencks told us about the Ponemah Bell...

...and then invited us to ring it.

Lots of people from the tour lined up. Young and old took turns and sometimes rang it together. It took some strength! Grimaces of the first few who tried to ring the bell, and then their grabbing on tightly with both hands signaled that ringing this bell wasn't as easy as it looked. We could not see the bell, but the full notes of its melodic tolling were hypnotic and memorable, if just for a few minutes.

The bell sat on a platform far above us, out of view.

Is it too far-fetched to suggest that perhaps the bell clamored to be heard once again? And, that we, equally needing to hear the sound of *the* bell that beckoned our ancestors to work so many decades ago, obliged it?

Built 150 years ago, the Ponemah Mill was the largest fabric mill in the Northeast U.S. during its construction. In 1924, four thousand looms were propelling Ponemah to historic levels of production. My grandparents and their large family had arrived at a time of great promise and influence. The Ponemah Mill certainly loomed large in my mother's life and memories. Its century of impact will continue to course through the lives of Taftville's descendant families like ours. ∎

Reflections

Toward the end of her life, when my mother and I talked about her weaving work, she never mentioned how humidly hot or noisy the Mill was, though she lost part of her hearing in one ear. Instead, she told humorous stories from her mill days, expressed how much she loved weaving all kinds of fabrics, and speculated about why she out-produced many other weavers.

My mother's success as a weaver was not complicated. Besides "paying attention" and learning the craft of weaving, she told me she always tried to be nice to people, a trait she had learned from both of her parents. As a result, her bosses looked after her and the loom fixers often repaired her looms ahead of other weavers.

Underneath her kind and pleasant exterior, though, my mother's will was as strong as steel. Clues to her perfectionist nature and competitive spirit were sprinkled throughout my childhood. She was a good softball batter, an ace croquet player, and a consistent winner in any card game.

She talked about playing lots of stickball in the Taftville streets when she was a kid and probably took advantage of the public croquet course once located where the Taftville Fire Station sits today. The card games she favored were popular through much of her lifetime.

My mother was a proficient lifelong learner. A good listener, she was receptive to hearing about approaches that might improve the way she did things. I expect that during her weaving years, especially early on, she became a sponge around more experienced and skilled colleagues.

Here she is during a 2002 visit to my home, on her way to winning the croquet game against three other players half her age. My father, whom she adored, had just died the prior autumn, but she looks very focused, doesn't she?

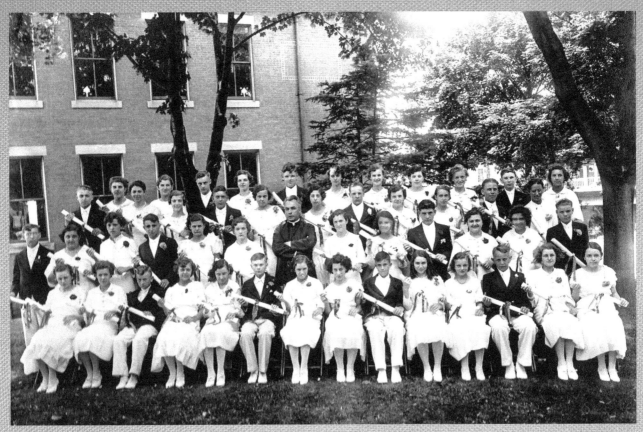

Class of 1935, Sacred Heart School, Taftville, Connecticut.
My mother Gabrielle Picard is in the top row, fifth person from the left, and next to the left tree fork.

A photo of my mother's 8th grade graduating class appears to the left. Like the other twelve children in her family, my mother did not attend high school.

This bothered her. She would often express to us her embarrassment about this lack of education, never acknowledging her weaving skill or other attributes, and also ignoring my father's comments that education and intelligence were not the same.

On one occasion when she was lamenting this perceived shortcoming, my father told my sisters and me how important Mom's income was to them in the late 1940s. When Dad returned from WWII, he earned $30 per week as an apprentice carpenter, while Mom was typically bringing in double that amount, thanks to the piecework differential at Ponemah. They lived on his income and built their house with hers. Dad looked a little sheepish while he told us this, but in both their eyes I saw pride.

For more than half my life, my image of my mother was based on my everyday experiences growing up. I saw a woman who spent her days efficiently making meals and desserts like her delicious apple pie, doing dishes and laundry, cleaning the house, and running errands once she learned how to drive. That was what I thought mothers did. That was who I thought she was, though she would often say how she hated most of these housekeeping chores! This was one of the clues I missed about who she really was.

Today, I latch onto any way to know her better. I so wish I had known her when she was weaving fabric at the Ponemah Mill or dancing on the excavation dirt.

How excited she must have been in the late 1940s that earnings from the job she loved were funding the house my father was building for them.

In the sunset years of Mom's life, she told us often with a sparkle in her eyes that she had wanted four daughters and got three. She said she was grateful. Unlike many other kids we knew, my sisters and I were assigned only a few housecleaning chores when we were growing up, and for those we received an allowance. She also insisted on paying us for helping her with spring and fall cleaning.

My mother voiced clear expectations when we were growing up. Her job was to be a wife and mother. Our job was to go to school, learn, and get good grades. And we did, partly because she helped us with homework. She did say often she wanted us to enjoy our childhood because hers had been cut short. "Go out and play" was a daily request from her.

Though generous in many aspects in rearing us, she didn't hesitate to discipline us when she felt we needed it, re-using the corporal punishment techniques from her childhood. As I entered my pre-teen years, I recall being in conflict with my mother a lot. Let's just say my sins reported in the confessional were loaded with instances of "I talked back to my mother."

The three daughters of Gay and Mike.
College graduations: Bernice (1972), Donna (1980), Cindy (1973).

As I look back on it now, I don't hold those swats of the strap against her, as it was typical of the times. Dealing with children and teens, who at times wouldn't do what she wanted, or as quickly as she wanted, frustrated her. It probably reminded her of dealing with her siblings when she managed the Picard household in Taftville. She and my father tried to teach us to think independently, yet be respectful. Sometimes that was a challenge for all of us!

Once I married, she became a friend rather than a mother. The change surprised me, but it shouldn't have. I think she felt she had done her job, the best she knew how, and I was on my own. She always helped upon a request, but never interfered.

After Dad died in 2001, she revealed she had wanted to return to work after I was born. Upon thinking it over, she had relented to my father's logical persuasion. She would stay home and take care of me—and her future children. I remember being stunned as she told me this. In her 81-year-old eyes there was a sadness. She left an important part of herself in that gigantic brick building in Taftville.

Maybe that is where she was, back with her looms, when she slowly washed dishes while staring out the kitchen window. Once in the 1960s, when I was sixteen, she spoke of Ponemah. Her melancholy voice caused me to suggest she might return to work. Her response in monotone, "It's too late." I recall making one more pitch. But, Ponemah was in decline. She knew she could not regain that blissful slice of time from the late 1940s.

I recognize now that Gabrielle Picard Janovicz was a woman with exceptional talents. In some ways, she was a preview of the women to come—the many women who would work for the money AND for the intrinsic rewards, while juggling work and home lives.

My mother was a weaver in her heart of hearts, but also a taskmaster, organizer, patient teacher, supporter, gentle medic, and sewing genie, to name a few. Her sewing passion when we were growing up reflected her love of fabric.

Sewing transferred some of her creative energy into making clothes for all the females in the family, including our dolls. And, just as she learned sewing skills from her

Some of the doll clothes Mom sewed. ▶

forebears and her own efforts, my sisters and I absorbed the fundamentals from her, and then refined our know-how with more experience and education. At one time, I was sewing half my wardrobe and nearly majored in clothing and textiles. My sister Cindy took a class in pattern making that proved immensely useful over many years.

I comprehended rather late in my life that Mom and I were far more similar than different. Clarity can be bittersweet. My eclectic career has gifted me a rainbow of skills, challenges, and an ongoing sense of achievement. My mother was a good listener, but I could go on and on about my work adventures. She never tired of hearing whatever I wanted to share with her.

My mother had hoped I would become a teacher. It was not something I would have chosen for myself, but serendipity sometimes selects us, doesn't it? A manager of mine recommended me, in mid-career, for a training position in the company where I worked. It turned out to be such a rewarding stretch of my work life that training became a service offered by my own small business later. So, Mom did get her wish for me.

It seems to me that my grandmother Eugenie Duhamel Picard imprinted some of her children with her own indomitable spirit.

For a woman of her time and despite bearing seventeen children, Eugenie's "essence" shaped my mother, who in turn, imparted some of her traits to her three daughters.

The WALKTOBER tours of the Ponemah Mill helped me visualize the place where my mother created all sorts of cloth—from blankets to coffin linings, and parachute material to a fine gossamer fabric that lined the wings of gliders.

Walking in my mother's footsteps illuminated me. For most of her life and mine, I didn't understand what an "expert" weaver my mother was, how valued an employee she was, and how she thrived in her job. I'm glad I know this now. ■

◀ *Gabrielle Picard Janovicz, 1945.*

▲ Skaters Bernice and Cindy.
Ford's Pond in East Great
Plains, Norwich, circa 1957.

▲ Gay, Mike,
and Bernice
on her first
birthday, 1951.

Cindy, Donna,
Bernice
snuggling
in our blue
bedroom,
circa 1960. ▶

▲ Donna
with Babcia
(grandmother)
Mary Janovicz,
circa 1961.

◀ Bernice and
Cindy getting
a swing push
from Dad,
circa 1955.

Mom with
Cindy and
Bernice in Easter
garb, April 1958.
(Mom expecting
Donna any
moment!) ▶

◀ Bernice,
Cindy, and
cousin Paul
with Tippy.

Epilogue

Home Sweet Home.

In March 1950, Mike and Gay moved into the house they built together. My father, a union carpenter, went to work at a construction job Monday to Friday, usually returning about 5:15 p.m. each night. My mother devoted herself to home matters and kept things running smoothly. During the 1950s, they welcomed three daughters.

Once we got a television, Mom or Dad would turn on the TV after supper and the two of them would sit and watch the evening news on CBS, anchored by Walter Cronkite. Many evenings after the news, my father would read a magazine like *Popular Mechanics* or

◀ *My sister Donna in the little car, circa 1963.*

Mom's Singer Sewing Machine. ▶

head to his cellar workshop, where magic occurred as far as we were concerned.

My father loved to "putter" downstairs in his basement work area, often using "treasures" he found at the local junkyard to test out his ideas. He is probably most famous, with our cousins and neighborhood kids, for "the little car" he built from scratch.

My mother's equivalent free time joy radiated from the Singer sewing machine they bought for her around 1960. I remember my mother's delight as

Cindy, Christy, Donna, Don, Peter
buggy riding, circa 1960.

Mike and Gay after Church, 1966.

Dad on the tractor improving
his truck driveway, 1965.

Uncle Roger, Aunt Mickey, and
daughter Gayle, circa 1950.

Aunt Ida and her daughter
Lena, circa 1965.

Cousins Don, Connie, Stevie, Michael on the
front porch of the farmhouse, circa 1951.

Picard cousins, circa 1975. Counter clockwise beginning with Aunt Pauline in center: Billy, Sally, Norman, Susie, Leo, Doreen, Richard, Betty Lou, Sheila, Roger. ▶

she got acquainted with her new piece of equipment. Mom tried out each capability of the "zig-zag" model. After that, she became a regular customer of area fabric shops, and all our wardrobes expanded.

My friends at school thought my family lived out in the sticks. Located on a plateau at one of the highest elevations in Norwich, our extended family compound was uphill a mile from the main road in the Bean Hill area. We saw my father's relatives on "the hill" every day or two, and had a ready supply of playmates between my cousins and kids our age living nearby on the street.

It was a glorious place. The family land offered ample acreage to roam and explore, but surrounding that were also pastures and woods as far as you could walk, in the era before deer ticks began to spread Lyme disease.

The countryside was filled with diversions and we enjoyed every one of them, with our parents when we were younger, and on our own from 'tween years on. We rode our bicycles and conjured up imaginary places. The hammock became our spaceship and the sand pile

◀ *Bicycle brigade in front of Uncle Tony and Aunt Albina's house. L-R: Christy, Cindy, friend Barbara, Bernice.*

our cities. Every season tickled our senses, pleased our palates, and kept us fit. We so loved berrying, nutting, skating, sledding and searching for pollywogs. During summer vacations, we honed our skills in horseshoes, softball, badminton, cards, and board games.

On Sunday afternoons, when my parents had free time, they liked to visit with family—and family liked to visit them. On my mother's side of the family, we were particularly close to our Picard cousins in Taftville.

In the good weather, my dad frequented the Waterford Speed Bowl. My mother wasn't fond of the noise and dust filling the air at stock car races, so she usually stayed home with Donna and reveled in a quiet day to herself. Cindy and I donned our white racing hats with blue goggles before we left home. Dad and the two of us sat in the stands near the final turn, munching on peanuts and Cracker Jacks and rooting for our favorite drivers.

On really hot summer days, our family would pile into the car and head for Wildwood Park on Lake Alexander in Dayville. Our relatives used to kid us

Mom operating the riding mower, 1980s.

Gabrielle and Michael Janovicz with family, circa 1989. I think MaryLynn is in this photo, too! Standing: Gay, Bernice, Chris, Cindy. Seated: Mike, Stephen, Wayne, Donna, Bill, Diana.

House under construction for Donna and her family, 1988.

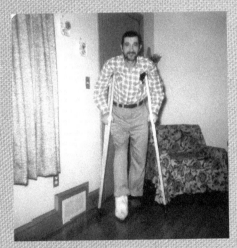

Dad on crutches, early 1980s.

The house after a snowstorm, 1970s.

Friend Theresa and Gay. Aunt Vee's birthday party, 2006.

that we always got there late, like we were crazy or disorganized. Actually, Mom and Dad liked to arrive at the lake as others were starting to leave, so that we had the place to ourselves in the calm of the sinking afternoon sun. I can still picture the rafts, waterwheel, and slide, as well as the blue popsicles carried by the concession stand.

On the way home from Wildwood we'd stop at Deary Bros., a favorite restaurant. (My detailed memories are of the early days, before Donna joined our family.) My mother would just shake her head as she watched Dad, Cindy, and I inhale the foot-long hot dogs loaded with mustard, relish, and raw onions. While we gushed about how tasty the hot dogs were, Mom quietly enjoyed her grilled cheese sandwich; for her, the ice cream was the main draw. When dessert time arrived, Dad chose his usual vanilla, Mom preferred strawberry or coffee, I ordered chocolate chip, and Cindy favored black raspberry. The ride home seemed a lot shorter as the textures and flavors melted in our mouths.

It brought immense satisfaction to my parents that all three of their daughters learned to play the violin. Aunt Albina, who lived right across the street, was a conservatory-trained violinist. She offered to give my sisters and me free lessons. So, for many years you could hear the

◀ *Aunt Albina, circa 1943.*

sounds of symphonies and exercises emanating from our house. All three of us young ladies played in the school orchestra. My sister Cindy and I remember the elegant brocade dresses Mom sewed for our concert attire—so we'd look our best.

Over the years, my mother avoided dealing with items like checkbooks, but after managing looms at the Ponemah Mill, no piece of equipment intimidated Mom! She would watch someone demonstrate how to use it, or she'd study the directions and try things. One year, my dad decided he and my mother had mowed around all the large rocks for the last time. He used his backhoe to dig out and remove every large New England boulder from the lawn. As you can see, Mom helped him with his project.

In the 1970s, my mother would finally see one of the important results of her choice to leave her weaving job and concentrate on raising a family. One by one, her daughters completed high school at the Norwich Free Academy and then achieved a college degree, with immense financial help from Dad working long hours as a foreman in the construction of the Millstone Nuclear Power Station in Waterford, Connecticut. I felt Dad was ruining his health during those

Mike and Gay kissing.

Jeanne, friend Evelyn, John and Rollie.

Mom, Dad, cousin Sally, Aunt Pauline.

1945 - 1995

The daughters of
Michael and Gabrielle Janovicz
request the pleasure of your company
for an informal luncheon and gathering
in honor of
our parents' Golden Wedding Anniversary
on Sunday, the twenty-fifth of June
nineteen hundred and ninety-five
at twelve o'clock noon
Tamarack Lodge

50th Anniversary
Invitation, 1995.

Dais: Uncle Jean Paul, Mike, Gay, Aunt Vee.

Mike and Gay cutting the cake.

Mike and Gay heading home after the festivities.

Cousins Monica and Stevie.

Sister Alphonsia and
brother Jean Paul.

years of seven-day workweeks, but Dad maintained that it was his choice. He didn't want any of us to deal with debt following college. When we expressed concern, he would point out that he might never have another chance to rake in four times his hourly rate on a Sunday. The added income fed my parents' retirement nest egg as well.

College wasn't a given for any of us. My dad sat me down one day when I was in my third year of high school and he told me he wasn't sure they could afford to send me to college. So, when I did attend, I took my opportunity seriously, and I expect my sisters did as well, as we knew my parents had sacrificed to send us. That being said, I suspect the degrees meant even more to my parents, and especially my mother.

Mom chose a handsome gold frame display with three connected 5 X 7 sections that held the college graduation photos of her daughters. She parked it on a prominent shelf in her kitchen, where she could gaze on it everyday and visitors would notice it. As the baby boomer generation of the Picard/Duhamel family came of age, many of our cousins also pursued college and

Aunt Florence, Mike, Diana, Stephen, Gay, circa 1987. ▶

advanced degrees. So, it took another generation, but our grandmother Eugenie finally got her wish.

After college, my sisters and I married, and three grandchildren were born. Once all their daughters left home, Mike and Gay really enjoyed the additional free time.

My mother discovered reading novels, especially historical romances. She was on the lookout for them and her beloved jigsaw puzzles each time she and Dad went hunting for bargains at yard sales—a passion of theirs.

As the years passed and the relatives aged, Mom helped to care for some of her siblings when they became seriously ill: her brother Ralph, sister Angela, and finally sister Florence.

My parents brought Aunt Florence to their home to live. Mom wanted to care for the sister who had once taken good care of her, after their mother Eugenie died in 1930.

Within two years, though, Mom couldn't manage the situation any longer. Alzheimer's is a terrible disease; it afflicted several in Mom's family. In her younger

◀ *Mom with grandchildren Diana and Stephen, circa 1988.*

Granddaughter MaryLynn ready to hit a home run in Little League, circa 1997. ▶

It was Valentines Day in 1938 or 1939 when we got hit with one of the worst snow storms in years. Mike insisted on bringing Gay a Valentine box of chocolates so he enlisted me to help him dig through a four foot snow drift across the road about where his driveway is now. With chains on the car and weight in the trunk he plowed through the drift and the rest was down hill. Naturally he did not want me to go with him so he was on his own, but made it to Taftville. I'm sure Gay was surprised but happy to see him. and can tell you more about that day. I have no idea how or when he got home.

Tony

That picture of Mike and I in uniform is the only time we saw each other during the war.

A remembrance from Uncle Tony, shared at the 50th Anniversary Celebration for Gay and Mike, 1995.

February 1944.

Dad enjoying the construction of his third family house, circa 1988.

Mom, thrilled with her gifts on Christmas Eve, 2006.

years, Mom had cratered once from exhaustion, and recognized she was on the verge of it again. I know my mother was heartbroken; she hated to place Aunt Florence in a nursing home.

On the cusp of his retirement, Dad needed open-heart surgery. It went well and he bounced back quickly to all his former activities. Dad had hinted for years that he wanted to spend part of his retirement building a house for one of his daughters—and he did exactly that.

In 1990, when he was finishing the inside of the house he built for Donna and her family, Dad was diagnosed with prostate cancer. He successfully battled it for several years.

My parents reached their 50th Anniversary in 1995. Though Dad wasn't feeling his best, I think they enjoyed the

Gay and Mike, 50th Anniversary, February 1995.

celebrations we planned for them.

Our immediate family celebrated at Donna's house on the actual date in February, followed in June by a nice gathering of extended family and close friends.

A second open-heart surgery in the late 1990s brought some complications. The years around the new millennium were difficult for my parents. In September 2001, the same week as 9/11, Dad lost his battle with cancer. His death was a terrible loss. Mom was now on her own, but fortunate for her, she had raised three daughters who loved her and looked after her. Those are the same years I really got to know her.

My mother Gabrielle spent a cold January weekend in 2009 in the hospital with pneumonia. She seemed to be improving, and I thought she was going to pull through. Mom was unusually happy through most of that weekend illness. Each of us had a chance to visit with her, and for that we were grateful.

My sister Donna later told us about a surreal moment during their final visit. Mom lit up like a schoolgirl in love. She leaned over to Donna, and with sparkling eyes she whispered, "I am going to meet my husband soon."

We believe she did … ■

Appendix

Gabrielle Picard Janovicz, 1946

Acknowledgements

This book resulted from a diversion in my writing plan. Early in 2017, I was conducting research for the sequel to *Until the Robin Walks on Snow*, but illnesses in our household and an unexpected trip intervened in the January to May period—and unlatched my schedule.

Serendipity slipped through the sliver in this doorway. She kept whispering to me that another opportunity was brushing my arm. By July, I found myself yearning to publish a book about my mother and her family. I realized two articles I had already written could serve as the base of the book.

The question was: could I finish writing it and publish by Thanksgiving or so. Then, I could swing back to my "Robin" sequel in January 2018? Here's where all my project management experience contributed. Yes, I believed it was possible, if I could find the right graphic designer to create both the cover and internal design of my highly pictorial narrative.

So, on August 1 of this year, I became a "hermit" and began to expand upon the articles I had written about the WALKTOBER tours of the Ponemah Mill I attended in 2004 and 2014. My original concept was to double the existing text and expand the photos by a third. I contracted with a graphic designer in the second week of September.

Well… books have a mind and heart of their own. They nudge you gently, this way and that, towards content and method you could consider. Authors will tell you this phenomenon really happens, often in revision. All I can say is, thank you muses and family in the astral plane! Writing this book about my mother turned out to be more of a challenge, but even more joyful than I expected.

In order to compress the time to publication, I needed the staff at various organizations to respond more quickly than usual. I am appreciative for their pronto help and for their enthusiasm about my project. For assistance with historical information and/or digital vintage photos I would like to thank these organizations: the Norwich Historical Society, the Otis Library, the Windham Mill Museum, the Rhode Island Historical Society and its Museum of Work and Culture, the Kheel Center at Cornell University, the Taftville Fire Department, and the Library of Congress.

The WALKTOBER tours of the Ponemah Mill, sponsored by the Last Green Valley organization directly influenced the richness and depth of this book about my family. I am so indebted to them and the tour leaders (the late Rene Dugas and Tim Jencks). If you live in the CT-MA-RI area, and don't know about the autumn WALKTOBER events, check the schedule for next fall when it is posted on their website. Treat yourself! Explore the terrific restaurants and B&B accommodations in eastern Connecticut and spend 2-3 days immersed in glorious historical and cultural outings while the foliage colors are painting the landscape of the Last Green Valley.

The community-minded actions by the owners of Onekey, LLC remind me that there are business people out there who persevere and creatively find solutions to benefit us all. It took years for Onekey, LLC to secure the level of funding needed to return life to these beautiful Ponemah Mill buildings. They permitted so many tours of the Ponemah Mill while their conversion project was in process or stalled. They may never fully understand how much it meant to the descendants of Taftville and the Ponemah Mill's employees. My eyes are watering as I write this... Thank you from my heart.

To those granting me permission to use their photos in my book—I thank you so sincerely. My book is far better, thanks to your generosity: Estate of Rene Dugas, Sr., Susan M. Schroeder, Robert "Red McKeon" & Family, the Jean Paul and Pauline Picard Family, the Anthony and Albina Janovicz Family, and Starshine Photographics. A special thank you also to Karen Faiola, who connected me with one of these photo owners when time was short.

My expert reviewers accomplished what I needed them to do, review and correct any errors in the historical and Ponemah building/tour related facts. Thank you so much Dale Plummer and Tim Jencks for your close review of my manuscript and for providing additional information of interest to me. That you read the manuscript and decided you wanted to contribute a promotional blurb for the back cover was gratifying. Thank you.

The Trumbull Wednesday Night Writers reviewed the pieces about the 2004 and 2014 tours I took. Group members, via their feedback, helped me refine the content as they evolved into articles. I have benefitted so much by my membership in this group, and I hope the members over time realize they touched this piece with meaningful feedback that has lived on as part of this book's words.

I would like to acknowledge Tim Jencks once again, for arranging my interview with Robert "Red" McKeon, his wife, and their daughter Karen. What a warm welcome they gave a complete stranger. I felt like I had known this family my whole life. We talked, we laughed, exchanged photos, and swapped information. I learned some fascinating new things, which landed in the book. It didn't get lost on me that we sat in the same home where my mother's stellar boss from the 1940s had lived. I am so appreciative to the McKeon family for meeting with me.

A handful of relatives helped me with bits of information, feedback, and photo identification or provision, mostly with short notice. My sincere thanks to my sister Donna, nieces Diana and Mary-Lynn, nephew Stephen, Aunt Vee, Uncle Tony, and cousins Susie, Sally, PJ, Monique, and Lena. Your input made a difference. I would also like to thank a Facebook Taftville group member, Estelle Thibeault, who helped our family identify an individual in a wedding photo that appears in the book.

The most fascinating aspect of genealogy is that the memory reservoir keeps releasing its treasures. It never disappoints. Aunt Rollie and Aunt Pauline—how many wonderful conversations we have had in recent years and weeks. Thank you both for all the time you spent with me, sharing factual information, family history, and stories about the time when you or family members worked at Ponemah. When you read the book, you will see just *how much* you helped me tell my mother's story—and our family's story.

My sister Cindy helped me *before* this book was conceived and also while it came together. A few years back she took the time to scan hundreds of photos in our family's photo albums. That scanning saved me untold hours and I am so grateful to have tapped into this useful family bank of history. She also took a few photos to be used in the book and spent time brainstorming with me to ensure I didn't forget something important in telling this story. Thank you so much,

Cindy, for all this and for that initial alert about the 2004 WALKTOBER tour. Attending that event was the kernel of this book!

Remember the graphic designer I mentioned hiring in September? What a gift she has been as a collaborator in my short duration project. Diane King is highly skilled technically, but also artistically. She has brought beautiful and thematic touches to the conceptual design and layout of my book. She understands layout sequencing, but also project priority sequencing. She thinks flexibly and has worked diligently to try to meet my expectations as a customer. Diane was definitely the right graphic designer for this project!

My editor, Natalie Schriefer, is one of those congenial, smart, and insightful people we all want to work with on writing projects. I am grateful for the thought she put into her two rounds of feedback on my manuscript, catching the little things, while providing high value comments, with relatively quick turnaround. I am particularly indebted to Natalie for gently making her pitch twice that I might want to refine the sequencing of my story. As a result, I was able to weave a finer fabric on a stronger frame. ∎

Gay... I'll always remember you eating apples. How you loved them! I guess you still do.

I also know you'll never forget the evenings we had warm donuts and cold milk. You would be sitting at the table writing to "Mike" as he was in the service at the time. Those were the days.

From the handwritten remembrance of Rollie, 50th Wedding Anniversary of sister Gay and Mike, 1995.

Photo Credits

Please do not reproduce any photo contained in this book without first contacting the owner or holder of a photo listed below. The vast majority of photos were sourced from the Michael and Gabrielle Janovicz Family Archive (too numerous to list) or the collection of Bernice L. Rocque, as indicated. Please contact the author at the email address on the back of the Title Page to request permission to use photos from either of these two sources.

PAGE viii: Taftville Mill and Village. Courtesy of: Kheel Center, Cornell University.

PAGE 1:   Ponemah Mill Building No. 1, 2014. ©2014-2017 Bernice L. Rocque. All rights reserved.

PAGE 5:   Taftville Mill and Village. Courtesy of: Norwich Historical Society.

PAGE 10:   Simplified Picard/Duhamel Family Tree – 3 Generations. ©2017 Bernice L. Rocque. All rights reserved.

PAGE 11:   The Earliest Settlers of Quebec City. ©2017 Bernice L. Rocque. All rights reserved.

PAGE 11:   Le petite histoire de la paroisse de SAINT-THEODORE-D'ACTON, cover and page 17. Le Soeurs de St-Joseph.

PAGE 15:   The Change of Shifts. Photo by Jack Delano, 1940. Courtesy of: Library of Congress.

PAGE 33:   Ponemah Mill Building No. 1, 2014. ©2014-2017 Bernice L. Rocque. All rights reserved.

PAGE 34:   Annotated Aerial Map of Taftville, the Ponemah Mill, and environs. From: Dugas, Rene L. Sr. Taftville, Connecticut and the Industrial Revolution: The French Canadians in New England, Book II, page 5. Permission to use from: The Estate of Rene Dugas, Sr.

PAGE 35:   Gabrielle Picard Janovicz, in front of Ponemah Mill's Main Building, 2004.
The former residence of the Picard family on South A Street, Taftville, 2004.
Both photos ©2004-2017 Bernice L. Rocque. All rights reserved.

PAGE 36:   Departing the Taftville Fire Station, 2014.
Intersection of Providence St. and North 3rd Ave., 2014.
Both photos ©2014-2017 Bernice L. Rocque. All rights reserved.

PAGE 37:   The major fire at the Sacred Heart Church, Taftville, April 1956.

The remains of Sacred Heart Church, Taftville, after the 1956 fire.

Both photos courtesy of: Taftville Fire Dept.

PAGE 38:   The author, at the display of her 2014 blog article, Taftville 150-Year Celebration, 2015.

The 1910 Fire Truck of the Ponemah Fire Company No. 1, 2015.

The engine cover of the 1910 Fire Truck of the Ponemah Fire Company No. 1, 2015.

Fire equipment stored on the 1910 Fire Truck of the Ponemah Fire Company No. 1, 2015.

All four photos ©2015-2017 Bernice L. Rocque. All rights reserved.

PAGE 39:   Sunday Mass at Ponemah Mill, circa 1956. Courtesy of: Otis Library, Norwich, CT.

PAGE 40:   Ponemah's Executives lived on the hill near the end of North 3rd Avenue, 2014.

This Ponemah building housed the medical office, 2014.

Both photos ©2014-2017 Bernice L. Rocque. All rights reserved.

PAGE 42:   WALKTOBER tour group approaching the "front door" of the Ponemah Mill, 2014.

©2014-2017 Bernice L. Rocque. All rights reserved.

PAGE 43:   The courtyard behind Building No. 1, 2014. ©2014-2017 Bernice L. Rocque. All rights reserved.

PAGE 44:   Above the power generation area in the "L," 2014.

The water intake area at Ponemah Mill, 2014.

Inside Ponemah's administration building, 2014.

All three photos ©2014-2017 Bernice L. Rocque. All rights reserved.

PAGE 44:   The train track extension near Ponemah building No. 2. Courtesy of: Tim Jencks.

PAGE 45:   View of the Shetucket River, 2014. ©2014-2017 Bernice L. Rocque. All rights reserved.

PAGE 45:   Interior renovation in the administration bldg, 2014. ©2014-2017 Bernice L. Rocque. All rights reserved.

PAGE 46:   Original mill flooring, 2014.

The south tower staircase of the Main Building, 2014.

Third floor, Ponemah Building No. 1, 2014.

The Ponemah Mill's ceiling groove design, 2014.

All four photos ©2014-2017 Bernice L. Rocque. All rights reserved.

PAGE 47:   Staircase to the fourth floor of Building No. 1, 2014.

South tower door to the fourth floor, Building No. 1, 2014.

Main Building 4th floor looking LEFT (southerly) from south tower entry, 2014.

Main Building 4th floor looking RIGHT (northerly) from south tower entry, 2014.

All four photos ©2014-2017 Bernice L. Rocque. All rights reserved.

PAGE 49:   Draper Northrop Loom.

Close-up of a Bobbin Battery.

Both photos courtesy of: Otis Library, Norwich, CT.

PAGE 49:   A Draper loom shuttle. From: The Northrop Loom: Serial 1764, Edition 1. Sourced from: University of Arizona.

PAGE 50:   Looms and the Mist. Untitled Photo by Jack Delano, 1940. Courtesy of: Library of Congress.

PAGE 51:   James J. McKeon, 1952. Courtesy of: Robert "Red" McKeon and Family.

PAGE 53:   Main Building 4th floor landing, 2014.

South tower doors looking towards staircase, 2014.

Fourth floor looking towards north side, 2014.

All three photos ©2014-2017 Bernice L. Rocque. All rights reserved.

PAGE 54:   Bathroom entrance, 2014.

The bathroom's sink area, 2014.

Both photos ©2014-2017 Bernice L. Rocque. All rights reserved.

PAGE 55:   The bathroom's toilet area, 2014.

The fifth floor of Building No. 1, 2014.

Both photos ©2014-2017 Bernice L. Rocque. All rights reserved.

PAGE 55:   The Ponemah Bell. Courtesy of: Tim Jencks.

PAGE 56:   Left - Giant window across from the fifth floor staircase, 2014.

Center - Facing the giant middle window, Fire Chief Jencks talks about the Ponemah Bell, 2014.

Right - Giant window along the fifth floor staircase, 2014.

All three photos ©2014-2017 Bernice L. Rocque. All rights reserved.

PAGE 57:   Mom relaxing and thinking, 2002. Courtesy of: Susan M. Schroeder.

PAGE 57:   Mom planning her next croquet move, 2002. ©2017 Bernice L. Rocque. All rights reserved.

PAGE 60:   Some of the doll clothes Mom sewed. ©2017 Bernice L. Rocque. All rights reserved.

PAGE 65:   Picard cousins, circa 1975. Courtesy of: Jean Paul and Pauline Picard Family Archive.

PAGE 67:   Aunt Albina, circa 1943. Courtesy of: Anthony and Albina Janovicz Family Archive.

PAGE 69:   Granddaughter MaryLynn ready to hit a home run in Little League, circa 1997. Permission to use: Starshine Photographics, Sprague, CT.

PAGE 82:   Ponemah Mill. Courtesy of: Kheel Center, Cornell University.

PAGE 87:   Bernice L. Rocque at NFA Book Expo, 2014. ©2014-2017 Bernice L. Rocque. All rights reserved.

Norwich, Conn. Ponemah Mills.

List of Sources Consulted

Allen, Frederick Lewis. *Only Yesterday.* Harper & Row, 1964.

Ancestry.com. Available at: https://search.ancestry.com .

Benedict, Judith and Rolf Diamant and Nadine Gerdts and Rosemary Wells. *Working Water: A Guide to the Historic Landscape of the Blackstone River Valley.* Rhode Island Department of Environmental Management, 1987.

Bessette, Claire. "Ponemah Mill transformation could define next century of Taftville history." *The Day,* May 6, 2017. Available at: http://www.theday.com/article/20170506/NWS01/170509497.

Choiniere, Paul. "Ponemah project could bring Taftville to new heights." *The Day,* May 7, 2017. Available at: http://www.theday.com/article/20170507/OP04/170509662 .

The Bulletin. Norwich, CT. http://www.norwichbulletin.com .

Dugas, Rene L. Sr. *Taftville, Connecticut and the Industrial Revolution: The French Canadians in New England,* Book II. 2001.

Dunwell, Steve. *The Run of the Mill: A Pictorial Narrative of the Expansion, Dominion, Decline, and Enduring Impact of the New England Textile Industry.* David R. Godine, 1978, pp. 133-134.

Eastern Connecticut Association of Realtors. "The Challenges of Mill Redevelopment: Ponemah Mills – Norwich, CT." October 27, 2014. Available at: http://www.easternctrealtors.com/assets/files/extras/PonemahMills.pdf .

FamilySearch. Available at: https://www.familysearch.org .

Hackett, Peter. "World Famous Northrop Loom Had Its Roots at Small Farm in Hopedale Area." *Sheltered from the Wicked World: Stories and Pictures from Hopedale's Past.* Available at: http://www.hope1842.com/drapernorthroploom.html .

Kheel Center, Cornell University. http://www.ilr.cornell.edu/library/kheel-center .

The Last Green Valley. WALKTOBER 2017. Available at: http://thelastgreenvalley.org .

National Volunteer Fire Council (NVFC). "Robert 'Red' McKeon Receives E. James Monihan Director Award." May 5, 2014. Available at: http://www.nvfc.org/robert-red-mckeon-receives-e-james-monihan-director-award/ .

The Northrop Loom: Serial 1764, Edition 1. University of Arizona, On-Line Digital Archive of Documents on Weaving and Related Topics. Available at: https://www2.cs.arizona.edu/patterns/weaving/monographs/ics1764.pdf .

Norwich, City of. Office of the City Clerk.

Norwich Historical Society. http://www.norwichhistoricalsociety.org .

Norwich Street Directory: Containing A General Directory of the Citizens, Street Guide, Classified Business Directory, Street Directory, New Map, Record of the City Government, Institutions, etc. New Haven, Price & Lee Company, 1924-1948.

Otis Library, Norwich, CT. http://www.otislibrarynorwich.org .

Read, Eleanor B. *Norwich: Century of Growth. Part I: The Mill Bell Tolls.* Franklin Press, 1978.

Read, Eleanor B. *String of Pearls – Cotton in Connecticut.* Norwich Heritage Trust, 1990.

Rhode Island Historical Society, Museum of Work and Culture. http://www.rihs.org/museums/museum-of-work-and-culture/ .

Rocque, Bernice L. "Walking in the Footsteps of My Mother: Inside Taftville's Ponemah Mill." November 16, 2014. Available at: http://3houses.com/walking-in-the-footsteps-of-my-mother-inside-taftvilles-ponemah-mill/.

Rocque, Bernice L. "Walking Weekends give one reader and her family a chance to walk in the past of Ponemah Mill." *The Norwich Bulletin*, October 13, 2005.

Les Soeurs de St. Joseph. *La petite histoire de la paroisse de Saint-Theodore-D'acton.* Saint-Hyacinthe, Arthur Douville, V.G., le 5 mars 1942.

Smith, Greg. "Firefighters to be inducted into Hall of Fame." *The Bulletin* 225, April 4, 2009. Available at: http://www.norwichbulletin.com/x549593632/Firefighters-inducted-into-Hall-of-Fame.

Stave, Bruce and Michele Palmer. *Mills and Meadows: A Pictorial History of Northeast Connecticut.* Donning Co. Publishers, 1991.

Taftville Fire Department. "History of the Taftville Fire Company #2 Incorporated 1917-2007." Available at: http://www.taftvillefire.org/History.html .

TCORS Attorneys. "Construction cleared to begin on first phase of Ponemah Mill renovation." *In the News*, March 11, 2016. Available at: https://www.tcors.com/construction-cleared-begin-first-phase-ponemah-mill-renovation/ .

Wauregan and Quinebaug Company Records. *Weaving Piecework Rates* and *Weaving Weekly Pay Rates*, 1943 Payroll & Wage, Box 206, Folder no. 145-1. Thomas J. Dodd Research Center, University of Connecticut Libraries.

The Windham Textile and Mill Museum, Willimantic, CT. www.millmuseum.org/ .

United States Census Office, Department of the Interior. *Statistics of Power and Machinery Employed in Manufactures: Reports of the Water-Power of the United States, PART I.* Washington, GPO, 1885.

Wisniewski, Chris. *The Hurricane of 1938: Norwich Remembers the Storm of the Century.* The Bulletin, 2013.

Topoquest. USGS Map Name: Norwich, CT. Available at: http://www.topoquest.com/map.php?lat=41.57552&lon=-72.11028&datum=nad27&zoom=4&map=auto&coord=d&mode=zoom-in&size=m .

In addition to the sources listed, personal interviews, and various quick reference tools such as thesauri and English language usage guides, maps, and French-English dictionaries provided information.

About the Author

Bernice L. Rocque is a writer, educator, family historian, and avid gardener. Her second book, *The Ponemah Years: Walking in the Footsteps of My Mother* is nonfiction: equal parts biography, history, memoir, and family portrait. The book centers on the author's journey to better know her mother, a weaver in the 1940s at the famous Ponemah Mill in Taftville, Connecticut.

The author grew up in Norwichtown, Connecticut in the surroundings described in her first book, *UNTIL the ROBIN WALKS on SNOW*, a novella based on a critical event in her father's family: the birth of a micro preemie in 1922 and the determination of her family and the midwife to save him.

Ms. Rocque has authored numerous business articles associated with her work in libraries, training & development, and project management. Articles she has written about her family have appeared in *Good Old Days and Family Chronicle*.

Her newest book, *The Ponemah Years...* evolved from attending the Last Green Valley's WALKTOBER tours of the Ponemah Mill in 2004 and 2014, and subsequent articles published in the *Norwich Bulletin* and on her Official Author Website www.3Houses.com .

You can connect with Ms. Rocque at her Official Author Website, www.3Houses.com, on Twitter @UNTILtheROBIN and Facebook at Bernice.L.Rocque.Author. If you read and love *The Ponemah Years... or "Robin,"* the author would welcome a short review from you on Amazon, Barnes & Noble, and/or Goodreads.

CPSIA information can be obtained
at www.ICGtesting.com
Printed in the USA
BVHW02s0027150618
519143BV00006B/18/P